DO-IT-YOURSELF
PLUMBING AND HEATING

DO-IT-YOURSELF
PLUMBING AND HEATING

by

HAROLD KING

PAPERFRONTS
ELLIOT RIGHT WAY BOOKS
KINGSWOOD, SURREY, U.K.

Made and Printed in Great Britain by Hunt Barnard Printing Ltd, Aylesbury, Bucks.

ACKNOWLEDGEMENTS

Research by Elizabeth A. King

Thanks and acknowledgements to the following companies for help and assistance:

Microbore Merchants Ltd (heating suppliers)
Wednesbury Tube Co (tube and fittings)
UCAN Ltd (fittings)
Key Terrain Ltd (cold-storage cisterns, rainwater goods)
IMI-Range Boilers Ltd (hot-water cylinders)
Econa-Parkamatic Ltd (waste-disposal units)
Glynwed Foundries Ltd (Leisure sinks and baths)
Finrad Ltd (skirting convectors)
Myson Group Ltd (fan convectors)
H. Mear and Co (heating calculators)
T.I. Radiation Ltd (Smoke Gobbler)
Agaheat Appliances Ltd (boilers)
Chaffoteaux Ltd (boilers)
Satchwell Controls Ltd (heating controls)
Robinson Developments Ltd (solar-heating systems)
Trent Valley Plastics Ltd (insulating products)

and also to Aubrey Taylor, mechanical-services engineer, for reading MSS and offering useful comments.

CONTENTS

LIST OF ILLUSTRATIONS

I

HOME PLUMBING AND HEATING

Modern methods and materials have brought plumbing and home heating jobs within the scope of any competent handyman or handywoman.

There is a natural reluctance on the part of many people to tackle jobs incorporating the elements of fire and water. Nevertheless, with care and confidence, making sure you have the right tools and materials and checking and rechecking at every stage, plus being clear as to what you are doing, there is nothing really very complicated. High labour costs and the difficulty of getting the right type of help make it more essential to tackle this type of job.

"Skill" no longer needed
You no longer have to be adept with stocks and dies, to thread and join heavy galvanised barrel pipework; lead-burning is another skill that has been displaced, with simpler and neater methods of connection.

Slim copper, plastic and stainless-steel tube, easy-to-use fittings, plastic and glass-fibre storage cisterns and copper hot-water cisterns are the modern plumbing front-line products.

You can, up to a point, marry new materials in an older plumbing system, but more often than not it pays to update; rip out the old and replace with new.

Planning is all-important. A plumbing or heating system needs care in determining the layout, based on your domestic needs, in terms of both storage and hot-water capacity and heating.

To an extent, plumbing and heating are interdependent. Similar techniques and materials are used, and the domestic hot-water requirements are supplied by the boiler in modern heating systems.

There is little point in installing a new heating system without updating the boiler, or in installing a new hot-water cylinder with an antiquated heating system, so before replacing any appliance and circuitry first check the entire installation.

Often sluggish water flow, and brownish sludge from taps points to heavily calcinated or lime-scaled pipework, restricting the bore and oozing rust!

Heavy barrel pipework and festoons of exposed lead-work are less than attractive. Modern materials are neater and easier to conceal. Lead also has the disadvantage of being more difficult to repair, in the event of burst pipes, since this requires a high degree of skill. However, a burst is at least evidence of poor insulation of exposed pipework—and here prevention by proper lagging is always far better than cure.

Major Jobs

What may appear to be a formidable task of replumbing or installing a heating system can be tackled by stages, following a workplan. Inspect your plumbing system. If you have a galvanised cistern in the loft there is no need to discard it if it is still serviceable. However, never connect copper directly to a galvanised cistern or electrolytic action will occur, causing corrosion and eventually a possible flood!

However, if there is any sign of deterioration, scrap the old cistern and replace it with a PVC or glass-fibre one, which, properly installed, will never need replacing.

The old cistern can merely be pushed to one side of the loft; often these are put in during construction of the house before the roof is fitted and there is sometimes no easy way to remove it. (You can, however, use a sheet saw or a hacksaw to cut this up—but this can be laborious —and heavy on blades!)

The hot-water storage arrangements are often fulfilled by a clumsy and inefficient galvanised tank, connected by heavy iron barrel pipe. This, too often, occupies a disproportionate amount of space in an airing cupboard. A modern, highly efficient hot-water cylinder will be much more effective and far more economical to run.

Both domestic storage and hot-water systems should be of a size sufficient to meet the household's present and future needs.

An old-fashioned boiler may not only be inefficient and not particularly decorative, but occupy far too much space in the kitchen—always an area of premium space. Modern, high-output boilers are neat, attractively cased and take up very little space. They can be housed beneath cupboards, on walls, in the loft, the garage and even out of doors, liberating valuable room.

A hybrid arrangement of old and new radiators is not a good thing and will almost certainly be a false economy. Old, heavy, cast-iron radiators, for example, may not be of sufficient output to meet the needs of a properly designed system and are no substitute for the neat modern design of radiators or other heat-emitting appliances— such as skirting radiators and convectors, both natural and fan.

Integrating a change-over can be done in careful stages to avoid household dislocation. Never embark on more than you can do at a given period. Avoid shutting off water supplies for other than the shortest time possible.

So remember; plan ahead, for adaptations made later may result in a less efficient system and cause much greater dislocation.

Plan for any kitchen appliances you might later fit— such as a plumbed-in washing machine, a water heater or a dishwasher.

When planning to update a plumbing system, decide whether the bathroom and kitchen layout of plumbing, furniture and appliances need rethinking; this can affect the arrangement of pipework. This is also the time, to minimise dislocation, to consider fitting a new WC suite, bath, wash-hand basin or bidet.

Planning Permission
You have to inform the local authority of any plans to replumb the home and to conform with model water-

board regulations, but this would not apply to, say, re-placement of a cracked wash hand-basin or a damaged WC.

For rerouting and redesigning the layout you must pro-duce a plan for council approval. This has to include all detail, including pipework and stopcocks. You must also show the existing layout to provide a comparison.

On a bungalow, a simple plan drawing will suffice. With a house, the full house elevations must be shown.

New homes

A new home may sometimes be available 'off the peg' without central heating, which helps to cut the purchase price and gives you leisure to install your own system as funds permit.

With the growing use of system building—where homes are built using pre-made modules from a factory range, but having all the qualities of a 'conventional' home—this particularly provides an opportunity to integrate your heating system into the house at post-construction stage.

A frame home may require only a few days work for a small team to erect on a prepared site.

Extensions

Planning your pipe runs and layout for extra plumbing —such as additional bedroom handbasin and possibly a downstairs cloakroom—during the course of building can save time, effort and expense later on. Planning can take the form of temporarily fixing floor surfaces to provide easy access and minimum dislocation.

If holes have to be cut through walls or openings made in ceilings for example, to admit pipework, it is simple to provide these during building, rather than knock holes and lift flooring and other surfaces after construction, then have to make good.

Some modern kitchen units are provided with ducts or spacing behind to conceal pipework. Consider carefully any future pipework before fixing units finally into place, for it may not subsequently be easy to remove them.

Take account also of any possible extension to the house when planning heating or plumbing. For example, if a loft area is likely to be converted and utilised for a playroom, activity area or even a bedroom, the heating layout and its capacity should recognise these potential future needs.

A loft bedroom, for example, will need both heating and plumbing. In any use of the loft, apart from the broad structural and building requirements, you have to consider the best position for cold-water storage arrangements and related pipework distribution, so that this avoids, where possible, repositioning with a great deal of attendant dislocation.

Also thought has to be given to drainage and connection to the waste services when installing additional plumbing.

A common improvement is the provision of an added-on utility room, for it is often possible to extend the depth of the home. This may take the form of a conventionally built extension or a prefabricated structure which becomes an integral part of the home. This use may take over part of the function of the kitchen and require rerouting of the plumbing and the provision of fresh services. Underground waste drainage services may have to be extended and require strict adherence to both health and building rules.

It is best to discuss your intentions with the local authority before seeking formal permission, for this can often cut corners and prevent frustration and delay when plans are rejected because some vital point has been overlooked.

Often discussion with local officials will assist in arriving at the best and most economical way of tackling an approach, saving time and trouble for everybody!

A useful source of information in the UK is a visit to one of the various Building Centres, where advice, and a wide range of information is complete with a permanent display of plumbing, heating and other building and related products.

2

HOW A
MODERN PLUMBING SYSTEM WORKS

Water is an essential commodity in the home. A supply is needed for drinking and general domestic purposes, as well as a service for flushing away wastes. It follows that your domestic plumbing and drainage system should be efficient and well maintained.

It is possible for an average person to use as much as 900 litres of water a day. A bath takes about 90 litres, washing oneself about 20 litres, and even hand washing accounts for around seven litres. It follows that with the enormous consumption this represents, taking everyone's use into account, that water should be used with economy.

Cisterns
For domestic purposes, you are usually required to provide a cold-water storage cistern, generally in the loft, normally the most convenient place. This serves two purposes —first, if the supply to the home is interrupted for any reason, it provides a supply reservoir, and second, the supply acts as a buffer if at one time any large amount of water is drawn off by a group of households, leading to a temporary lowering of water pressure. The storage cistern can only replenish at a given rate, so this cannot place an undue strain on the supply services.

Also mains water comes in at a very high pressure able to cause wear on fittings and the bore of the pipes and likely to set up the noisy vibration of pipework known as 'water hammer'. Since most services in the home are

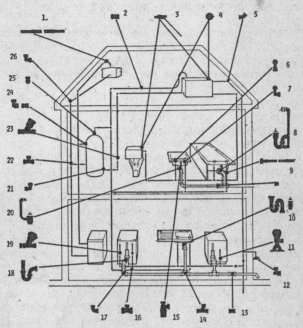

1. Schematic layout of typical plumbing and heating arrangements. Many of the basic pipework and waste fittings are shown. These pipework connectors are compression-ended. Items, left to right, are: 1, Copperbend (flexible connecting tube); 2, Straight coupler; 3, Ball valve; 4, Ball float; 5, Swept or obtuse bend (135°); 6, Straight swivel tap connector; 7, Right-angled swivel tap connector; 8, Combined bath trap and waste; 9, Copperbend; 10, 'S' trap; 11, Washing-machine connector; 12, Wall-tap connector; 13, Straight waste connector; 14, 92-1/2 swept waste tee; 15, Bottle trap; 16, Reduced tee-connector; 17, 90° knuckle waste bend; 18, Washing-machine trap; 19, Washing-machine adaptor; 20, Combined sink waste; 21, Angled male connector; 22, Equal tee-piece; 23, Stopcock; 24, Angled and straight female connectors; 25, Straight male connector; 26, Right-angled (elbow) pipe connector.

(Diagram courtesy of UCAN Ltd.)

served from the storage cistern this reduces both noise and wear. This is called an indirect system. A direct-to-tap system, met in some older properties, is generally not acceptable.

The kitchen and an outside tap are usually the only two services which may be connected to the mains—the kitchen to provide a supply of fresh non-storage water and the garden to provide the pressure necessary for a hose.

Supply pipe

Your responsibility for the domestic service is from beyond the water authority's stopcock, usually in the pavement outside the home. Sometimes these become covered during repaving or resurfacing of the footpath and it is a good idea to provide your own stopcock just on your premises to allow access for emergencies. There should, anyway, be a stopcock just inside the home where the supply enters to enable you to shut off the water.

It is recommended that the supply pipe should be buried at least 450mm (18 inches) deep—to be safe from garden implements and below what is called the 'frost line'. Usually a pipe of 15mm bore will provide the necessary supply. If, however, you live in a low-pressure water area or if the domestic demands are exceptionally large, a supply pipe of 22mm diameter may be necessary.

Existing supply services usually consist of lead pipe. Modern installations, or in circumstances where you may wish to replace the supply pipe, may use imperishable heavy-duty plastics such as butyl.

Rising Main

Once the service enters the home it is then called the rising main. You should fit your stopcock where it can be got to easily and quickly in the event of an emergency —more often or not under the kitchen sink is an optimum place.

A stopcock is defined as a type of tap with a non-return valve. This means that the water can flow only in one direction. If this is fitted the wrong way round, there

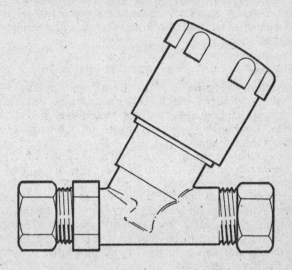

2. A Stopcock.
  This is the type you would use on the rising main.

can be no supply to the home. The direction of flow is shown by an arrow on the body of the fitting.

The purpose of the non-return valve is to avoid all possibility of pollution caused by back-flow of stale water to the mains.

After supplying the kitchen sink, the rising main should be routed as directly as possible to the storage cistern. The cistern has to be capable of being drained down faster than it can be filled, which means that the outflow pipe must be bigger than the inflow. Supply to the cistern (as to a toilet) is controlled by a float valve. This consists of a hollow plastic or copper ball, screwed on to an arm. The float rises with the water level and shuts off the inlet valve at a determined point.

As a further safety device, all types of cistern must be fitted with an overflow. Outlets for these should be in a conspicuous position to provide immediate indication of any failure on the part of the valve to shut down. This can sometimes happen because the water shuts off at too high a level. The ball arm is capable of some adjustment to correct this.

Hot Water

The cistern supplies a further storage appliance—the hot-water cylinder—which, in turn, may be linked with the central-heating system. This replenishes via an inlet near its base as hot water is drawn off from the top or crown of the cylinder.

It is advisable to fit a gate valve (a form of tap) in the supply from the cistern to the cylinder so that the latter can be isolated and drained down, fully or in part, when carrying out modifications, repair or maintenance.

The cylinder supplies hot water to the kitchen and bathroom. Cold water for the bath, wash hand-basin or bidet is supplied from the cistern. It is a useful refinement to provide gate valves in the supply pipework so that all these facilities can be isolated when necessary.

Drainage

The drainage system consists of two sections—that above and that below the ground. The above-ground system consists of waste services from sinks, WCs, wash hand-basins, baths and bidets. Drainage from gutters must be drained separately from the household drainage.

Traps, which contain water seals, connect the internal with the external drainage and prevent foul sewage air from percolating back into the home. There are two basic types of trap—the P trap and the S trap. These roughly resemble these letters. An S trap is taken out through a floor, while the P trap goes out through the wall. You can also have left-hand and right-hand connectors to go through side walls.

For baths, wash hand-basins, sinks and bidets there are two types of trap—the tubular or the bottle trap. These are made in shallow seal and deep-seal versions, the latter is required for wash hand-basins. If you fit a waste disposal unit in the kitchen, you must use a tubular trap

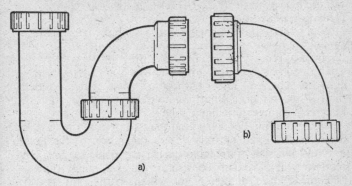

a)

b)

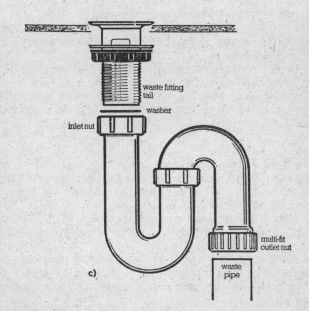

waste fitting
tail

washer

inlet nut

multi-fit
outlet nut

waste
pipe

c)

3. Different Types of Trap.
  a) A 'P' Trap. This comes out through the wall.
  b) A Trap to convert a 'P' Trap or a Bottle Trap to an 'S' bend.
  c) An 'S' or Tubular Trap. This is taken out through the floor.

rather than a bottle trap, because this is less liable to the formation of sediment.

While these traps provide the essential water seal between drainage and sewer connection, you can unscrew the base to remove sediment and débris.

Trapped yard gullies (outside the house) are used to connect kitchen and bathroom waste-water outlets, though in modern plumbing systems, usually only the kitchen is connected using a gulley.

New plumbing construction has to use a single-stack arrangement, sited entirely within the fabric of the home to avoid the risk of freezing up in very cold weather. The modern stack system consists of a soil stack pipe of 100mm–150mm diameter to which baths, toilets and basins are all directly connected. This also presents a more attractive house exterior, with cleaner lines.

The stack pipe vents to the atmosphere at a minimum height of one metre above the home, or where no noxious smell can get indoors.

A two-pipe drainage system, consisting of separate disposal into the sewer for waste water and foul water is common in older plumbing systems. The waste water was usually drawn into a trapped yard gulley via a hopper head.

Joints

Modern drainage and waste water systems consist of easy-to-use plastics (ABS or PVC). These are usually push fit, with an 'O' ring or similar seal, or are solvent welded. It is essential to observe the manufacturer's instructions in use or this may lead to trouble. With solvent-welded products, use only the make of cement specified by the manufacturer.

Modern plumbing and heating is easy to connect up, using modern copper pipework. Tube can be joined in two ways—with compression fittings or with solder fittings.

There are two types of the latter, one containing the solder, called a capillary fitting, and the other, without solder, called an end-feed fitting, where you apply solder to the mouth of the fitting.

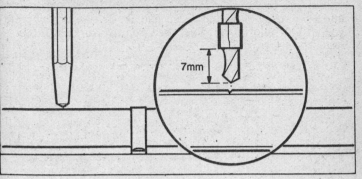

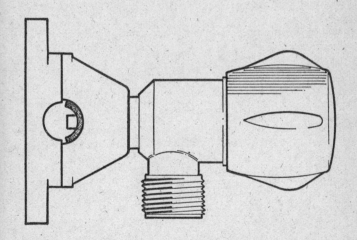

4. The 'Ucan' Quick Connector.
above—preparing the tube for Quick Connector:
left   —use a centre punch to dot-mark the position on the tube
right   —use a hand drill with a twist bit, preferably with a depth
            stop, to drill the hole
below—the 'Ucan' Quick Connector is then put on to the tube

A third choice for making connections where a branch outlet is required is the Ucan Quick Connector, where you drill a hole in the pipe, then clamp a branch fitting to it.

3

TOOLS AND TECHNIQUES

For any basic heating or plumbing work, you will need a small selection of tools. Make sure that these are the best you can afford, for good tools will not only help you to do a better job, but they will outlast cheap ones, which anyway are likely to give you less successful results.

Cutting and bending tubing

When cutting copper or stainless-steel tubing, you can use either a hacksaw or a rotary pipe cutter. The pipe cutter is more expensive but cuts tube quickly and neatly. It is not, however, suitable for microbore pipework—10mm diameter or below—as this leaves an indented rim which is difficult to remove and restricts the bore of the tube.

A standard hacksaw is between 255mm and 300mm long, and some are adjustable. A small or junior hacksaw will usually do the job just as well and is often easier to use, especially when working in a restricted space.

Copper tube is fairly soft, so a low-tungsten steel blade can be used. On stainless steel, you need to use high-speed steel blades which cost more but last longer. On large-bore pipe—above 15mm—use a 22-point or a 32-point blade. This indicates fineness or number of teeth to each 25mm length of blade.

Fit the blade with the teeth pointing away from the handle—usually, an arrow printed on the blade shows this direction. Slacken off the wingnut on the handle of the hacksaw before slotting on the blade, hand tighten, then tighten a full three turns.

When cutting, use a long and steady stroke at about

25

one stroke per second for low-tungsten blades, and around 70 strokes per minute for high-speed steel blades. Release pressure on the return strokes. Simply cut evenly and do not force the blade, or it will wear prematurely and quickly break.

Avoid starting a new blade in an old cut, for this can fracture the blade. Cut as squarely as you can, for an unsquare end may not give a watertight joint.

Always measure carefully, then recheck before cutting to avoid wasteful errors. Add the depth of the pipe within a fitting or the length will be short. For bends, add a little extra, and cut the tail of the tube accurately to length after bending.

A rotary pipe cutter is a good investment where you have a lot of tube to cut. The cutter rotates round the tube and is capable of a wide range of adjustment. Cutting is by rotating the cutter, around the tube, and progressively tightening a spindle until the pipe is cut through by its blade.

The indented rim around the cut edge has to be removed with a round file. Some cutters have a pointed blade at one end to remove this rim or burr.

You require both a flat and a rounded file for use with a hacksaw. The flat file is used to square the end of the tube and to chamfer the outside ends slightly to facilitate entry into the fitting. The rounded file is used to remove cutting burrs from inside the tube. The rotary pipe cutter produces a slight bevel when it cuts the tube.

For most purposes, you need only a pair of adjustable spanners to tighten standard plumbing compression fittings. For fittings used on cylinders or on boilers, a pair of heavy-duty wrenches may be needed, because these are fairly large. These can be hired. You may also require them when removing heavy rusted cast-iron fittings from old pipework.

Tube can be bent or cut and connected with angled fittings. Unless you require a very tight bend, it is best to manipulate the tube, using either a bending spring or a pipe-bending machine. Though a shallower bend will result, this has two advantages. It provides a more even water flow and there is less water turbulence at the joints

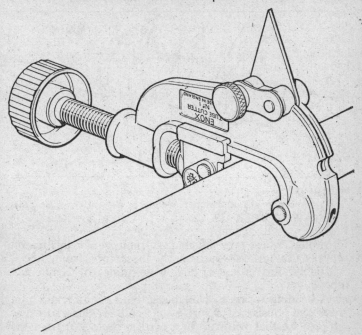

5. The Pipe Cutter.
  This is rotated about the pipe and the wheel is tightened slightly
  from time to time until the pipe is cut through.

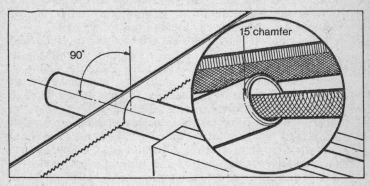

6. Cutting a Tube with a Hacksaw.

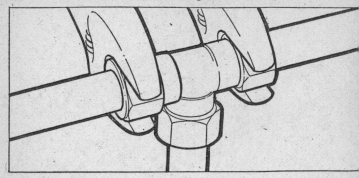

7. How to Tighten a Fitting.
  Two spanners are used simultaneously to prevent stress on other
  parts of the system.

of fittings, which may impair performance. For this reason
always use fittings—particularly those for 15mm tube—
sparingly; this is less critical with fittings of 22mm and
above.

A bending spring is available in both 15mm and 22mm
sizes and consists of a spring-steel coil. At one end it has
an 'eye' so that you can fix a cord to remove it from the
tube after bending. You can also use the eye with a screwdriver as a lever to 'unscrew' an over-tight spring. Insert
the spring so that its centre is in about the middle of the
bending position. Bend the pipe evenly against the knee
to form the radius required. If you overbend it slightly
then correct, the spring will come out more easily.

Plan your cuts in relation to connections carefully and
you will avoid wasting tube. However, it is difficult to
bend a piece of tube of less than 150mm–200mm in
length for there is little to hold. You can make up an
extension piece to your bending spring which enables
you to use these shorter ends of tube.

First, take a piece of tube the same diameter as that
being used and around 300mm long. File out the central
ridge or stop from a straight compression fitting. Attach
this securely to one end of the tube. To use, slide the
spring through the extension piece and fitting and into

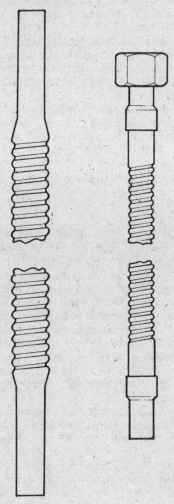

8. Two Basic Types of 'Ucan' Copperbend.
The one on the right connects to the tail of a tap.

the tube. Lightly tighten the loose end of the connection. It will be rigid enough to make a bend with a tail of pipe of only 75mm–100mm.

It is difficult to bend tube greater than 22mm in diameter with a spring, so you need to use a bending machine for larger bores. These are relatively costly to buy but are readily available on hire. Some plumber's suppliers will hire these out.

The machine does not use a spring but a former, called a shoe or slipper which is half rounded and when in place encircles half the tube. This shoe is pulled round a half-rounded former with the tube in place, forming a neat bend without kinking.

Another useful product is Ucan Copperbend, a flexible connector you can bend by hand.

Blow torches

You will need a blow torch if you are going to make soldered joints The modern butane or propane type is best, is easier to use and gives an even flame. (These are more satisfactory than the older paraffin or petrol blowlamps, which need priming and can be dangerous if not used with great care.) There are two main types—those with a disposable replaceable cannister and those with an exchange bottle. The latter are better on two accounts —the flame head is attached to a flexible pipe to the bottle, giving greater ease of use, and it is cheaper if you have a fair amount of work to do and can, of course, be used for paint stripping. However, these are rather more expensive than cannisters.

A flexible steel tape is needed to measure pipework. It is best to work in metric (most steel tapes are dual metric/imperial), since you will usually buy tube in 3-metre lengths. A lightweight portable vice with fibre jaws or a pipe vice is handy for holding pipe when cutting or manipulating. A pipe-bending machine is usually fitted with an engineering vice.

Plastic tubes

You can use PVC or polypropylene plastics, too, for cold-water supply only—provided these are not connected

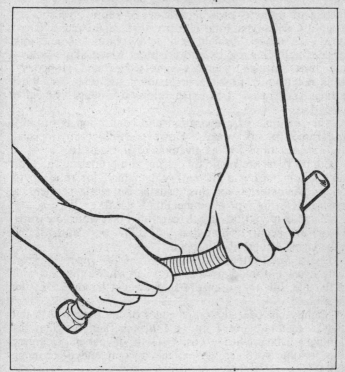

9. Using 'Ucan' Copperbend.

to a hot-water source, such as a copper cylinder, for example, which could cause the pipe to expand and possibly rupture, since plastics expand considerably at higher temperatures.

Plastics have superior insulation characteristics compared with metal pipes and are virtually condensation-free on the surfaces. They are not prone to form lime scale inside and are quieter and give improved hydraulic flow because of the smoother bore, which means that often a smaller diameter tube can be used. For example, 10mm diameter plastic tube can be used where 15mm copper or stainless-steel pipework would be necessary.

In an average domestic context, you will need about 30

metres of pipe to provide cold-water supply. Plastic fittings are usually a little cheaper than metal ones. There is a wide range—straight connectors, branch connectors or tees, reducing pieces and adaptors which allow you to use brass fittings, such as gate valves and stopcocks. It is not usually possible to bend plastic tube, so elbow fittings are used where there is a change of pipe direction.

The principle of preparation and connection is broadly the same for all makes. However, follow any special recommendations for the given make of product.

Connections are made by cutting and preparing the tube and jointing using a solvent-weld method for tube up to 50mm diameter. Over this, usually for waste services, a push-fit 'O' ring type of connection is usual.

As with any tube, check carefully that your measurements are accurate and that you allow the depth of the tube inside fittings at either end.

Use a fine-toothed hacksaw to cut the pipe squarely, with even, unforced strokes. You can square the end with a flat file, but try to ensure that the cut is correct in the first place.

Slightly chamfer the outer edges of the pipe with a flat file to facilitate entry into the fitting, then roughen the joining surface with abrasive cloth or paper. Degrease the mating surfaces, using the recommended cleaning fluid.

Brush an even coat of cement both inside the fitting and around the tube and immediately push the fitting on to the pipe. Hold in place for a few seconds then remove surplus cement. Leave the joint for about five minutes to set and then handle only with care. The weld reaches its full strength in about 24 hours. Solvent cement evaporates quickly and is highly flammable, so close the tin immediately after use and never use where there is naked flame.

Because PVC has a high rate of thermal expansion, do not site fixing brackets close to pipe joints, for this will impede longitudinal movement.

It is important to clip the tube at correct intervals (see table opposite) to ensure longitudinal freedom.

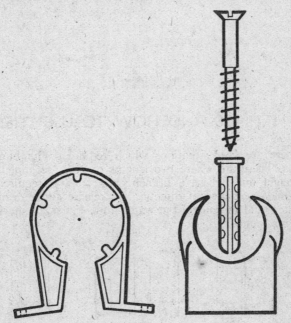

10. Two Different Sorts of Pipe Clip.

Installation intervals (mm)

bore (mm)	vertical	horizontal
10	1050	750
15	1800	900
25	2100	1050
28	2100	1050

Do not site plastics close to hot-water circuitry; allow about 75mm of air space so that the tube does not get hot.

B

4

FITTINGS AND HOW TO USE THEM

There are four situations which require a plumbing fitting. These are where two lengths of pipe are joined in a straight line; where a branch connection is required; to provide a change of direction; to release air or drain off water; and to control the water flow, either automatically or mechanically.

a)   b)   c)

11. Different Sorts of Straight Connector.
   a) Compression ended connector
   b) Female FI straight connector
   c) Male MI straight connector
These last two are used for connecting into a hot water cylinder, water heater or boiler.

The most common fittings are the straight coupling, for joining sections of tube; the branch connector or tee-piece, allowing a connection to be taken at right angles from a tube; the bent coupling or elbow, provided a tight, 90-degree angle or a shallower, slow bend.

Fittings are called equal or unequal. An equal tee is one where all outlets are of the same diameter. The tee-piece can have equal or unequal ends, to meet your needs.

The correct way to describe a branch connector is by

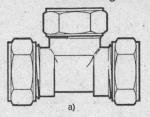 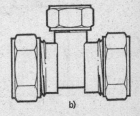

12. The Branch Connector or 'T' Piece.
   a) An equal 'T' where the outlets are of equal diameter
   b) A reduced 'T' (typically 22mm x 22mm x 15mm)

the two ends in turn and then the branch outlet. A 22mm fitting, with a 15mm branch outlet would be described as 22m × 22mm × 15mm.

There are also reducing sets, for couplers, compression, and for capillary fittings, which reduce down an outlet from a larger to a smaller bore.

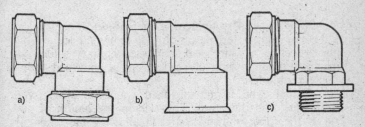

13. Compression Elbows or Bend Couplings.
   a) Coupling to provide connection for two pipes at right angles
   b) and c) Female FI Elbow and Male MI Elbow to provide connections for couplings into hot water tanks, boilers or water heaters

Fittings are a potential source of turbulence and may not look attractive if exposed. They are also expensive, so always use the minimum number of fittings possible. Rather than join two short pieces of tube with fittings, use one longer piece. The other piece may come in useful elsewhere.

There is a wide range of plumbing fittings to cover every situation. There are two basic types—the compres-

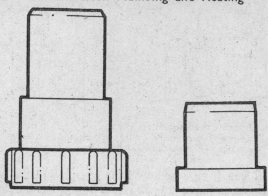

14. Reducers.
    left —a multi socket Reducer. Used more typically when adapting
          or extending existing system.
    right—an ordinary Reducer used more typically when constructing
          an entirely new system.

sion fitting, where by tightening the capnut of the fitting,
a brass or copper ferrule or olive is tightened around the
tube, effecting a water seal, and the capillary solder fitting, containing a ring of solder, or the end-feed fitting
which is solderless.

·A further type is the end-feed connector which you
make using a belling tool. This widens the mouth of one
end of the tube to form a socket, allowing the other, or
spigot end to be joined for an end-feed solder connection.
This is by far the cheapest way of connecting tube but
does need some skill and experience.

If you have never carried out any plumbing work before, it is best to use compression fittings, for these can
always be removed easily, and if there is any water seep-
age on a fitting this can usually be put right simply by
slightly tightening the fitting's locknut or capnut. However, always turn off the water and drain that part of
the system down when removing fittings.

Another type of fitting is the manipulative fitting. It is
seldom used domestically, for it needs special tools to
bell out the mouth of the fitting. The union is completed

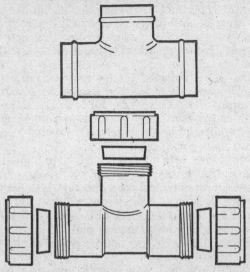

15. Different Types of Fitting.
  above—a capillary (solder-ring) fitting
  below—a compression fitting showing ferrules or olives

by tightening lock nuts. This type of connection is sometimes used for central-heating oil lines from the storage
tank.

Connecting compression fittings
When assembling a compression fitting, slide the capnut
then the cone or olive on to the tube, then push the tube
fully home, up to the stop in the tube. This is important
to provide a watertight seal. It helps to smear a little non-
toxic plumbing compound on the olive to consolidate the
joint. Check also that the tube is squarely cut and that
there are no burrs inside it to inhibit the water flow.

Tighten the capnut by hand, ensuring that the tube
remains firmly pushed home, then tighten a further $\frac{3}{4}$ of
a turn. This is adequate for tube of up to 28mm diameter.
When tightening, support the fitting on the body or on
the other capnut to avoid distorting the tube.

There are many makes of compression fittings and the cone or olive is not always satisfactorily interchangeable, so always use one of the same make. You can usually buy spares from plumbers' merchants and heating suppliers.

In some cases, threaded fittings are used, primarily on boilers, cylinders, water heaters, cold-water cisterns, and similar appliances. These are either male threaded or female threaded and may be used to reduce down to accept a smaller fitting or to terminate with a connector. The threads have to be sealed.

Two ways are with a gasket-seal compound or with PTFE tape. PTFE tape is very easy to use. Wrap this three times in an anti-clockwise direction (against the run of the thread). If you wind it the wrong way, the tape may shred and come adrift. PTFE tape both seals and lubricates the joint. Smear gasket seal lightly around the threads as an alternative. Do not use *either* on the threads of compression fittings.

An older, traditional way is with non-toxic plumbing compound smeared lightly around the thread and then a hemp, 'teased' into a thin string.

Where you are making a number of connections, it is easy to forget to tighten one. Either tighten as you go and check each fitting in turn or mark fittings for subsequent tightening.

Soldered joints

A piece of asbestos or asbestos mat is a wise provision at the back of the work when making soldered joints. Make sure that there is nothing which will easily ignite before lighting your blow torch. Set this to a hard, blue flame for best results. Butane flame is very hot—so keep hands well clear!

There is a reservoir of solder in a ring inside a capillary fitting. Check that the ends of your tube are cleanly cut and free from burrs and thoroughly clean the tube and the inside of the fitting with wire wool. There are, however, some makes of flux which do not require the mating surfaces to be burnished.

Apply a smear of flux to the joining surfaces. This

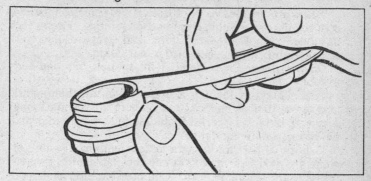

16. Using PTFE Tape.

prevents oxidisation which could weaken or nullify the solder bond.

Stainless-steel tubing is similarly treated but you need an 'aggressive' flux for jointing. This removes the oxide film which forms more readily than on other metals. These fluxes, available in both liquid and paste forms, usually contain an acid base. Ensure that excess flux is wiped clean after jointing, or corrosion may eventually occur.

Unlike compression fittings, it is best to join the tube and solder both ends in turn. If you attempt to solder one end without connecting the other end of the fitting, the solder in it will melt and you potentially have a poor joint. When making a joint with unequal tees, solder the largest end first.

After assembling the fitting, wipe off excess flux, make sure that the tube is pushed well home, and apply heat evenly to the mouth. Avoid concentrating this at any one point, for this can blacken and destroy the solder. Once a ring of solder appears completely around the mouth of the fitting, the union is complete. As a precaution, touch a piece of cored solder around the still-hot mouth of the fitting to consolidate the joint.

End-feed fittings are similarly prepared and assembled. Apply cored solder to the mouth of the fitting rotating it slowly until it will accept no more.

When using a belling tool to make a spigot-and-socket connection, use a similar method of jointing. Evenly bell out one end of prepared tube and prepare the ends, assemble and effect an end-feed solder union.

Do not disturb a soldered joint until it has had time to cool.

This method of jointing is useful when matching metric to non-compatible imperial tube. There are various adaptors and reducing sets available so that you can match pipework of different diameters.

If a tube has to be terminated temporarily or permanently, you can fit a stop end, available in both compression and capillary form. Compression stop ends consist of a brass disc which fits inside the body of the fitting and is closed off by tightening the capnut. On soldered fittings, it consists of a soldered cap which closes off the end of the fitting.

Tubing

Plumbing tubing consists of light-gauge hard-temper soft-drawn copper, stainless steel pipe or PVC and polypropylene tube. Tube diameters, with imperial equivalents, are as follows:

6	8	10	15	22	28	32	38	54	75	mm
$\frac{1}{4}$	$\frac{5}{16}$	$\frac{3}{8}$	$\frac{1}{2}$	$\frac{3}{4}$	1	$1\frac{1}{4}$	$1\frac{1}{2}$	2	3	in

However, you may need to join new pipe to an existing system. In some cases, you will need to join pipe of dissimilar bore.

The following are the sizes which are interchangeable.

15	28	54	mm
$\frac{1}{2}$	1	2	in

10mm will fit a $\frac{3}{8}$in pipe with a 10mm olive and $\frac{3}{4}$in fit a 22mm pipe with a $\frac{3}{4}$in olive but not the other way about. $\frac{3}{8}$in tube will fit 10mm fittings using $\frac{3}{8}$in olive, and $\frac{3}{4}$in tube fits 22mm tube using $\frac{3}{4}$in olive.

Generally, you will not have difficulty when joining waste services. Products such as Ucan waste fittings with a Multifit connector will connect practically any make of imperial waste fitting.

5

COLD-WATER STORAGE

When replumbing, it is wise to take a long, hard look at the existing cold-storage cistern, usually located in the loft, in order to provide the correct static 'head' or pressure of water needed to give the right degree of pressure at taps. Also, as a cistern is fairly bulky, this is the most convenient place for it. Running water, as the cistern refills, is less audible away from the main part of the home.

Storage cisterns have capacities varying from between around 250 litres to 350 litres. The choice depends on the demand for water, usually related to the size of home. A typical three-bedroomed home and a family of four needs a minimum storage supply of 250 litres.

An old galvanised cistern may be well past its best and it may be wise to change this. Modern cisterns are made either of PVC or glass fibre (more correctly glass-reinforced plastics or GRP) and are light to manoeuvre. These types of cistern have an infinite life and will not corrode or rot as may metal cisterns. Some PVC cisterns can be partially folded to go through a small loft opening.

Check the pipework connecting the cistern, for this, too, may need replacing. Plan all work with care so that you minimise dislocation of domestic water supplies.

You may be able to retrieve some of the fittings on the old cistern – such as the ball valve – though a float may sometimes become punctured and waterlogged. This simply unscrews, so it is easy to replace. Only use items in good condition.

When installing a new cold-storage cistern, sometimes incorrectly called a 'tank', it is sensible to plumb this as far as possible before installing it in the loft.

To remove the old cistern, check that you have all the tools you need to hand. Shut down the domestic water supply service by closing down the stopcock. Open the taps and flush toilets to drain the old cistern. Once drained down, you may have to scoop out a small residue of water at the bottom, for fittings are usually set above what is called the 'sludge line'. Iron fittings, if heavily corroded, may have to be heated with a blow torch and then removed using a large wrench.

Apart from providing a reservoir of storage, or 'potable', water in the home, the cistern also serves as a 'safety valve' for the hot-water cylinder. As heated water expands, this must be accommodated by an expansion pipe, taken from the crown of the cylinder and curved over the top of the cistern.

Hot water does not usually vent into the cistern, but such provision is necessary, for if the heated water were contained it could produce dangerous pressure and burst the cylinder.

The cistern should be plumbed for supply, with one or more outlets, and an overflow, in case the inlet valve fails at any time to operate and shut off supply. This overflow should be taken outside and clear of the house and be in a prominent position, so that it gives instant warning of any problem.

The mains inlet supply valve should be of a high-pressure type, actuated by a shut-off arm controlled by a ball which floats on the water and closes the inlet at a given height, called a ball float. The low-pressure type of valve is used for toilet cisterns, which are supplied from the storage source.

Dependent on the position of services and on water demand it can sometimes be useful to serve the cold make-up supply to the hot-water cylinder with a direct pipe from the cistern and provide a separate supply for the other services.

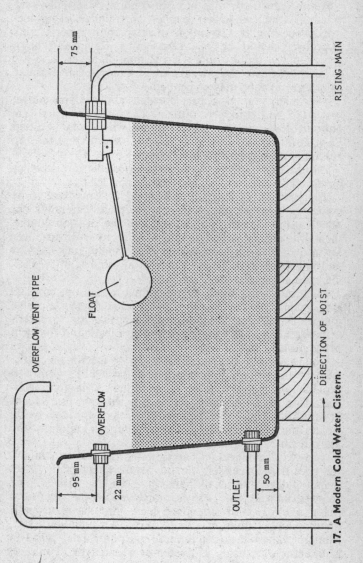

75 mm

OVERFLOW VENT PIPE

FLOAT

OVERFLOW

95 mm

22 mm

OUTLET

50 mm

RISING MAIN

DIRECTION OF JOIST

17. A Modern Cold Water Cistern.

Supply pipework, or the rising main, is usually provided in 15mm diameter copper or stainless steel pipework—but smaller (10mm) if plastic supply pipe is used. Overflows should be one size larger—22mm— than a supply pipe. Supply *outlets* in 22mm diameter tube are usually adequate but if there is exceptional demand, 28mm supply tube may be needed.

The inlet supply is best located about 75mm down from the top and the outlets 50mm–75mm from the bottom of the cistern. The overflow, which may be fitted in push-fit plastics should be about 100mm from the top and maintain a slight fall throughout.

Ensure that pipe runs, as far as possible, are level or have a slight fall, to overcome possible air locks.

The openings for the fittings in the cisterns have to be made so measure the positions of these carefully, dot punch using a centre punch, to keep the drill on course, then drill out. It is best to use a hole cutter or an auger bit in a hand drill, for a power drill usually runs too fast and will heat up plastics. Remove any burrs, after drilling, with a rounded file.

Inlet valves are fitted by tightening a lock nut on each side against plastic or fibre washers or possess a single nut which tightens the body of the fitting to the cistern wall. You can adjust the amount of projection of the stem of the fitting.

Connect a swivel compression tap connector on to the stem of the fitting. This contains a loose fibre washer to provide a watertight joint. The fitting is, in turn, connected up to the rising main. It is a wise provision to fit a gate valve into this pipework so that you can easily isolate the cistern while still maintaining a supply at the kitchen sink.

Tap-swivel connectors can be either angled or straight, the type used dependent on the arrangement of the pipework. Older patterns of ball valve, with a silencer pipe screwed into the base, are no longer approved because of the possible risk of siphonage back into the mains in a low-pressure situation, and possible pollution risk. Modern valves tackle reduction of water inlet noise in a different way, using a quieter overhead type of inlet.

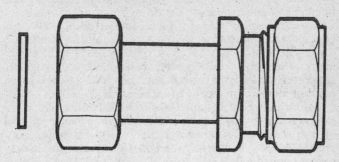

18. A Tap Swivel Connector.

The cistern outlet is fitted in thè same way as the inlet connector. This also has a backplate and one locking nut or two locking nuts and sealing washers tightened against the wall of the cistern. It is a sensible idea to fit a gate valve into the outlet pipework so that you can isolate supply to wash hand-basins, baths, cisterns and the like.

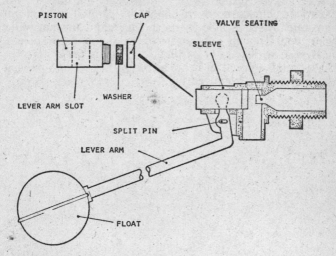

19. Typical Ball Valve Mechanism.

Overflow connections similarly screw into place and push-fit connections are made to the fitting.

Once the cistern is in place, make sure that it is adequately supported. PVC cisterns should be placed on three pieces of 50mm × 100mm timber, set at right angles across the joists. GRP cisterns must be continuously supported, or they may crack and then leak. A continuous piece of 19mm blockboard is suitable.

Before filling the cistern up, check all connections carefully. If during filling there are any signs of leakage, turn off the water and drain down the cistern. On no account try to tighten joints with water in the cistern, for it may rupture and flood.

You can slightly adjust the ball valve by carefully bending the arm. Valves of a diaphragm pattern possess an adjusting screw. This should shut off water at least 25mm below the overflow pipe. Test by drawing off a small quantity of water and checking that the valve shuts off on replenishment. After about a day, check again for any weeping of joints. If so, shut off supply, drain down and correct.

Provide your cistern with a lid to keep out dust. Blockboard or chipboard covers should be painted to keep out moisture. Make a hole in the lid to admit the hot-water vent pipe. Though lofts and cisterns should be insulated, it is wise to leave out insulation beneath the cistern, so that a small amount of heat can rise in winter and prevent the water inside from freezing.

6

DOMESTIC HOT WATER

The modern hot-water cylinder is far more efficient than the old-fashioned galvanised square tank, frequently unlagged and connected using heavy iron pipework and supplied with heat from a primitive boiler or heated by an immersion electrical heater—expensive in this relatively inefficient arrangement.

Though the modern cylinder may be fitted with an immersion heater as a stand-by, in modern plumbing practice, domestic hot water is usually provided as an integral part of the domestic central-heating system. On one make of boiler (Chaffoteaux Celtic) instant hot water is built in.

There are two basic types of cylinders—the *direct* in which the cylinder water is heated, drawn off and replenished with fresh water, and the *indirect* cylinder—which has an inner pipework arrangement called a calorifier through which heating water circulates. Another type of indirect cylinder is the self-priming cylinder, where the primary, or circulating water is separated from the secondary, or draw-off water, by an air bubble. If the water is heated beyond boiling point, the bubble will disperse and the two waters will co-mingle. The bubble will, however, reform on cooling.

It is necessary to choose the type of cylinder with care so that it corresponds with the heating system you intend to install. A direct cylinder is unsuitable, on its own, for use with central heating, for you would be drawing off the circulating heating hot water. Lime scale can readily form and corrosion can occur. However, a direct can be converted to an indirect cylinder by means of an element such as the Wednesbury Micraversion—resembling an immersion heater. Primary water circulates through this element, so that the two waters are separated.

For some types of heating system, such as those where heating water to the cylinder is pumped, the self-priming cylinder is unsuitable. A good modern system will employ a pumped primary, in which the circulating water is pumped by the boiler, rather than by the old-fashioned and uneconomic gravity or hydro-siphonic system, where water circulates by natural expansion and contraction through large-bore pipes (usually of 28mm diameter).

As hot water is part of the heating system in most cases, it is important that this works to optimum efficiency. With a pumped-primary installation, a high-recovery cylinder (one which reheats quickly) should be chosen.

A modern heating system can economically provide all the hot water needed in summer from the boiler. An advantage of an immersion heater is that it can provide hot water if the heating system develops a fault or is out of action for maintenance. It is also possible to link solar heating to provide most if not all your domestic hot-water needs during warmer weather and even boost energy during winter.

Hot water expands and rises, so is hotter at the top of the cylinder. The top is crowned to help hot water to rise and exclude air locks.

An average cylinder size is 915mm high×450mm in diameter. The bottom of the cylinder is dished upwards to provide strength and to prevent the formation of condensation. A cylinder should be stood on two firm pieces of timber so that air can circulate beneath.

A standard cylinder heats from cold in an hour to an hour and a half. A high-recovery cylinder takes only about half an hour.

Immersion heaters have a rating of around 3kW/h and should be connected using 4mm^2 cable. They are fitted with thermostatic devices allowing temperatures to be set between 49° C and 82° C. The usual setting for domestic use is around 60° C.

The two basic types of immersion heater are the single and two-stage patterns. The latter enables you to heat

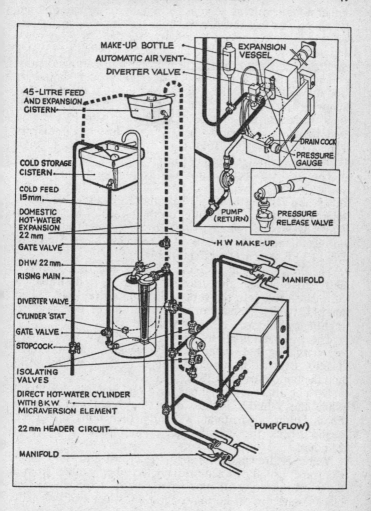

20. Schematic Layout for a Microbore Heating System.
Incorporating a hot water system also, for both a sealed and as open type of installation.

either a large volume such as for a bath, or a small amount of water, for washing or washing up. Immersion heaters are available in various lengths or 'reaches' to meet varying domestic water needs and sizes of cylinders. Water stratifies, so it is possible to heat it down to various depths.

The length of a full-sized immersion heater should be about two thirds of the cylinder depth. It is fitted by unscrewing the sealing plate from the immersion-heater boss. First seal the threads of the heater with PTFE tape and tighten it by hand, then against its sealing washers with a large wrench. Take care not to overtighten, for a thin-walled cylinder is easily ruptured.

Threaded connections are used to plumb in connections to a standard cylinder. Some have male threads and others are female-threaded. Seal these threads with PTFE tape before fitting. The outlet on the crown of the cylinder may have to be reduced down to accept a fitting of the correct diameter by means of a reducing bush. Similarly wind PTFE tape around the threads.

The lowest point of connection is for the cold-feed entry, to replenish the draw-off water. It is desirable to fit a gate valve into the supply line and a draincock called an MT (which stands for empty) fitting at the base, so that the cylinder can be easily drained.

The two next highest connections are for the primary or circulating hot water and are usually male-threaded. The top connection should be joined to the flow pipework, and the bottom to the return.

Do not attempt to tighten up a leaking cylinder fitting while the cylinder is full, or it may split and cause a flood. Drain down, tighten slightly, then refill and check again. Check the cylinder for sound joints after about 24 hours.

Water is drawn off through the crown and the expansion pipe, usually of 22mm diameter tube, is taken from a point on the draw-off pipe by means of a branch or tee-piece connector. In normal operation, water will normally vent only a short way up the pipe.

For a pumped-primary connection, tubing of 22mm is adequate. A gravity system requires connections of 28mm pipework. Draw-off and cold-feed supply pipework

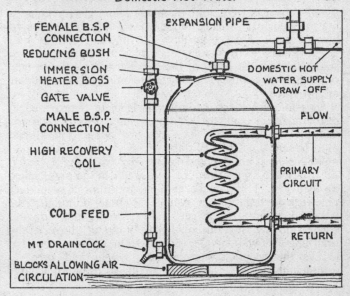

FEMALE B.S.P CONNECTION

REDUCING BUSH

IMMERSION HEATER BOSS

GATE VALVE

MALE B.S.P. CONNECTION

HIGH RECOVERY COIL

COLD FEED

MT DRAIN COCK

BLOCKS ALLOWING AIR CIRCULATION

EXPANSION PIPE

DOMESTIC HOT WATER SUPPLY DRAW-OFF

FLOW

PRIMARY CIRCUIT

RETURN

21. Layout of Typical Indirect Hot Water Cylinder.

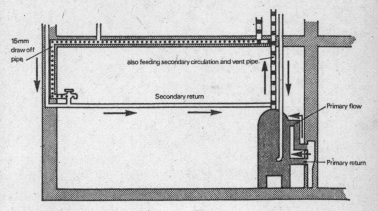

15mm draw off pipe

also feeding secondary circulation and vent pipe.

Secondary return

Primary flow

Primary return

22. How to Avoid a 'Dead Leg'.
   This can be done by fitting a secondary pipework installation in which water circulates all the time.

usually consists of 22mm diameter tube. The cylinder is best located in an airing cupboard, so that any dissipated heat is used. Always insulate a cylinder properly. You can fit a glass-fibre or mineral-wool jacket 'tailored' to go snugly around the body of the cylinder and tied with tape or straps. Increasingly, pre-lagged foam-surround cylinders are provided.

On some cylinders a small sealing plate is provided to enable a drain cock to be fitted. This is simply removed and the threaded MT cock screwed home. The thread must be sealed with PTFE tape.

Where taps are located some way from the cylinder, this can leave a great deal of cold water in the pipe, called a 'dead leg'. This can be avoided by fitting a secondary pipework installation in which the water circulates the whole time and never gets cold. The normal draw-off connection has an additional supply circuit above it and returning below it. Water drawn from a distant hot tap breaks the secondary circulation system and provides instant hot water without first having to draw off a large volume of cold water. See fig. 22.

7

KITCHEN PLUMBING

When replumbing in the kitchen, you need to consider such matters as the best layout and the provision of new kitchen equipment, and how it will fit in. Where possible, try to make use of existing supply and drainage services, subject to getting the best layout arrangements for your needs. It is a sound idea to work out the layout to scale using graph paper and pieces of card to represent kitchen units and appliances.

The type of kitchen sink you choose may have a bearing on the plumbing requirements. Kitchen sinks can be single or double-bowled, with left-hand, right-hand or double drainers. You also need to take into account supply to and drainage from appliances such as dish washers and washing machines.

Plumbing in follows a similar pattern to bathroom plumbing—fit taps and connect swivel connectors—straight or angled as need be—to the tap tails, cut and line up pipework connections before fitting a kitchen sink unit in place. This makes things much easier.

The choice of mixer taps or single taps do not require any change in plumbing arrangements. The separate tap tails connect to hot and cold water—the mixing is done in the body of the tap.

You can use a 75mm deep tubular or bottle trap on the kitchen waste outlet. Where a waste eliminator is to be fitted, you must, however, use a tubular trap, for this is less liable to sedimentation. A waste eliminator grinds waste into paste and disposes of this through the soil drainage system.

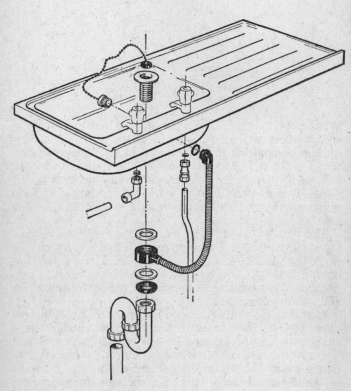

23. Typical Sink Plumbing.

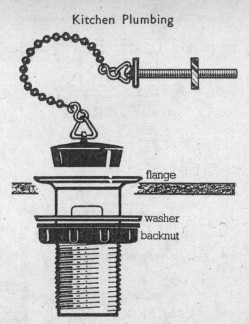

24. Detail of the Waste Fitting (shown without waste collar).

Your incoming supply can be taken to the kitchen cold tap and to serve a garden tap. The supply—called the rising main—15mm in copper and 10mm in PVC—is taken to supply the cold cistern, which, in turn, supplies water to toilets, baths, wash hand-basins and bidets, appliances and the hot-water storage system.

Ensure that pipes are clipped at frequent intervals to wall surfaces to cut stress and vibration, and that pipe clips are clear of plastic tube connections, so that expansion of pipework is not affected.

Washing machine
This can be plumbed by connecting, as required, a pipe from the cold-storage cistern and the hot-water cylinder. This depends on the requirements of the appliance.

To connect it is necessary to shut down water supply and make the connections. A stopcock should be fitted to

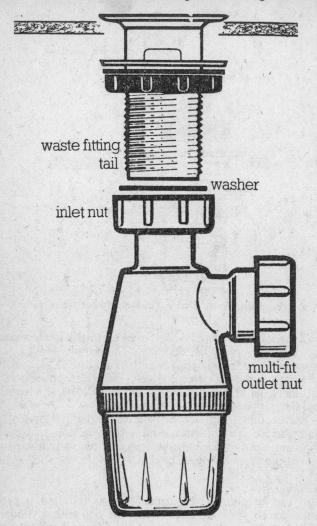

waste fitting
tail

washer

inlet nut

multi-fit
outlet nut

25. A Bottle Trap.
As used in a kitchen among other places. This must not be used
with a waste eliminator.

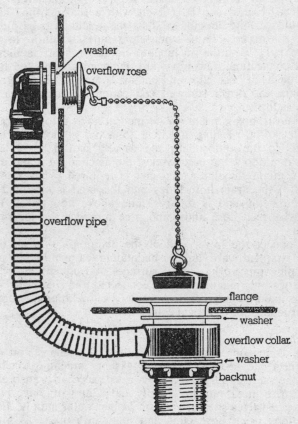

26. Combined Waste and Overflow System.

the supply taps and a short tail of 15mm pipe extended beyond. There are flexible pipes on the back of the machine to connect to. These are usually longer than are needed. Excess can be cut off with a sharp knife. They should be long enough to allow the machine to be pulled out for access. These connecting pipes slide on to the pipe tails. A little washing-up liquid or soap facilitates this connection. The pipes are tightened around the tube by means of hose clips and unions. Some machines possess fittings for direct screwed connections to male-threaded connectors.

An air break needs to be incorporated into the waste outlet of a washing machine to avoid siphonage. This vents to the atmosphere and usually should be at least 450 mm above the base level of the machine. A stand pipe of a minimum 38mm diameter is required. The crooked end of the drain hose loops into this, and is mounted so that the top end is some 800mm above floor level. The gap between hose and stand pipe provides the air-break vent.

Connect the lower end of the 38mm pipe to an out-side trapped yard gulley, maintaining a gentle fall and clipping pipework to wall surfaces at frequent intervals. The washing machine can be connected to a standard 13 A ring main supply via a switch. Follow manufacturer's instructions for electrical connection.

Dish washer

The connecting arrangements are very similar. You can connect the dish washer and washing machine together on the same supply service, via a tee piece or branch connector, using 15mm hot supply and 22mm drainage pipe. Fit gate valves so that you can isolate water supply. Connections using hose clips and union are made as for a washing machine. A separate drainage connection has, however, to be made. This can usually be made in 22mm pipework. You should allow a bend in the pipe to provide a water seal. Dishwashing machines should also be provided with a separate electrical circuit, which can be part of the 13A ring mains.

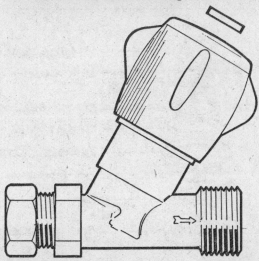

27. Washing Machine Adaptor.
This is a type of stopcock.

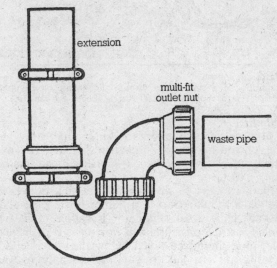

extension

multi-fit
outlet nut

waste pipe

28. Washing Machine Trap.

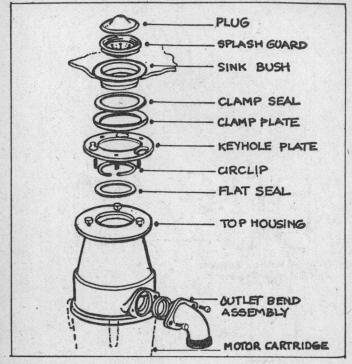

             — PLUG

             — SPLASH GUARD

             — SINK BUSH

             — CLAMP SEAL

             — CLAMP PLATE

             — KEYHOLE PLATE

             — CIRCLIP

             — FLAT SEAL

             — TOP HOUSING

             — OUTLET BEND ASSEMBLY

             — MOTOR CARTRIDGE

29. A Waste Eliminator.
The assembly of a sink waste disposal Econaunit or eliminator. This connects to the sink waste outlet (Econa-Parkamatic).

Waste eliminator

If you fit a waste eliminator, the sink outlet may need enlarging, or you may have to change the sink. However, Parkamatic offer a model which connects to a standard 38mm sink outlet.

The eliminator fits to the base of the sink outlet, and connects via a tubular trap to a 38mm waste pipe and a trapped yard gulley. An eliminator is simple to fit from the detailed instructions supplied. For reasons of hygiene, the outlet pipe should be taken below the water level so that deposits are not left. If you are discharging waste into a septic tank, this has to have a capacity of at least 5,000 litres.

The unit's motor is wired to a 13A switched power point.

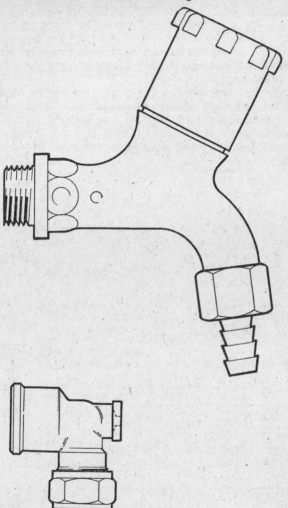

30. Utility or Outdoor Taps.
above—a utility tap
below—the type of connector used to join up an outdoor tap.
This should be firmly mounted to the wall.

A garden tap usually only requires a short pipework connection, via a branch or tee connection from the rising main. This usually means drilling into the kitchen wall to take out the pipe. You can do this laboriously with a sharp cold chisel and a club hammer, or a long-reach masonry drill pipe.

There are various types of outdoor taps, some of them threaded to accept a hose connector. The tap should be firmly mounted to the wall with a suitable fitting and lagged in winter, for if water freezes in a tap, it will push off from the fitting and possibly rupture the supply pipework.

8

MODERNISING AND REPLUMBING THE BATHROOM

All too often older bathrooms can be a disaster area in the home with poor space utilisation and festoons of out-dated cumbersome lead or iron barrel pipe. Apart from inefficiency of performance these may well be less than attractive. Equally valuable space may be taken by a dominant, galvanised hot-water tank and overlarge airing cupboard.

Modern bathroom appliances take less space and tidying up the supply and drainage pipework will give a much smarter and neater vista and make it easier to apply durable wall surfacings, such as ceramic tiles or vinyl wallcoverings.

It is, of course, necessary to disconnect water supply before you start on any replacing or updating work in the bathroom.

First, make a careful inventory of all the materials you need. New sanitaryware should be chosen with care and it pays to shop around. To make sure that the items you choose fit into the space available, it is useful to plan beforehand on graph paper.

If you are able to make use of existing supply and drainage pipework, try to ensure that the new equipment can be connected with the minimum of rerouting of these services.

Sanitaryware comes supplied with gummed paper edging, which affords protection during transit and fixing. Always leave this in place until the last moment and remove by soaking; never chip or scrape it off, or you may damage the surfaces.

Wash hand-basins consist of three types—the pedestal, where the basin rests on a centre column of vitreous china; the wall-hung basin, mounted to the wall by a fixing bracket; and the inset basin, built into horizontal surfaces, such as vanitory units.

Baths are made in enamelled cast iron, enamelled pressed-steel and acrylic plastics or glass fibre.

Modern baths are fitted with adjustable feet to level the bath and cause it to sit evenly on the floor. Plastic and steel baths usually have a wooden cradle support. Some plastic baths possess ribbed sections and do not require further support. Use a spirit level to ensure the bath is level. This provides the correct drainage fall at the sloped base.

WC pans terminate with a water-trap bend. These are called either 'P' or 'S' traps. The 'P' trap goes out through

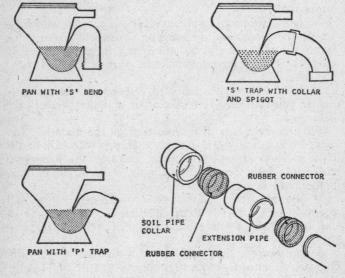

PAN WITH 'S' BEND

'S' TRAP WITH COLLAR AND SPIGOT

PAN WITH 'P' TRAP

SOIL PIPE COLLAR

RUBBER CONNECTOR

EXTENSION PIPE

RUBBER CONNECTOR

31. Various Types of Pans and Connections.

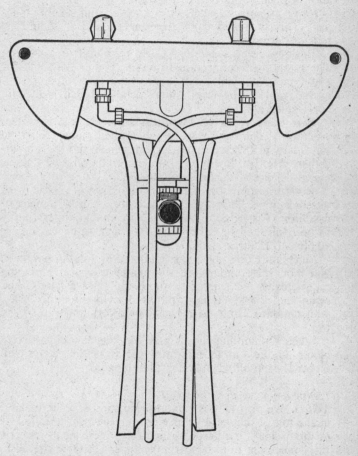

32. How to Cross Pipework Behind a Basin.

the wall, and the 'S' trap is taken out through the floor. Some pans are provided with separate china connectors, allowing a choice of P trap or S trap.

Never attempt to patch up a cracked and seeping toilet pan. This is a serious health hazard and it should be replaced at once.

Flushing cisterns are high-flush, mid-level or low-flush. The method of connection to a WC pan is the same for any type. An older, high-level cistern can often be removed and a low-level suite, usually much neater in appearance, substituted.

Two basic types of low-flush suite are the low-level washdown pan and the close-coupled suite. Siphonic suites are a close-coupled system which simply join together. Another low-flush, but less common WC pan, is the corbel closet which is wall-attached.

Modern cisterns are made usually either of plastic or of vitreous china. Older types of cisterns are usually made of cast iron. Cisterns are reversible to enable water supply to be connected to either side. Average water capacity is 10 litres to 12 litres.

Bidets may often be accommodated in a bathroom when you modernise and utilise the available space. Plumbing requirements are similar to those for a wash hand-basin. A hot and a cold supply is required to supply a mixer tap, with standard 32mm basin waste pipework and a deep-seal trap.

When replumbing run, if possible, the new pipework in alongside the old to minimise the time that water will have to be cut off when finally plumbing in.

Fitting a new wash hand-basin

To remove an old wash hand-basin, unscrew the locknut at the top of the waste trap, allowing the trap to fall clear of the basin. Use a basin wrench for preference to unscrew the connecting nuts beneath the taps. Unscrew the basin from the wall and unscrew the fixing screws on a base pedestal unit.

Connect up new taps by bedding these in a non-toxic plumbing mastic compound. Mastic is non-hardening and retains elasticity which helps to ensure a watertight seal.

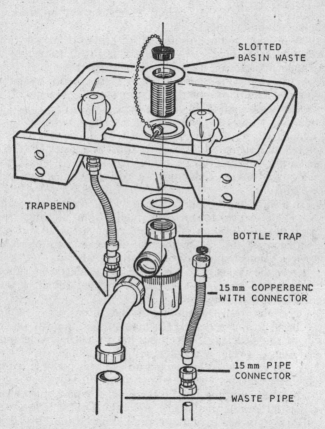

SLOTTED
BASIN WASTE

TRAPBEND

BOTTLE TRAP

15 mm COPPERBEND
WITH CONNECTOR

15 mm PIPE
CONNECTOR

WASTE PIPE

33. Typical Basin Connections.

Fit washers, usually supplied in polypropylene, between the 'top-hat' lock nut which screws on to the tail of the tap.

Next, fit a swivel tap connector, which effects the seal by means of a fibre washer; either angled or straight, dependent on the pipework.

To provide a neat, out-of-sight pipework connection, avoiding acute bends in pipework, fit 15mm tube bent to an angle and crossed over behind the pedestal

A useful product here is Ucan Copperbend, available with one end terminated in a tap swivel connection, or plain at each end. This can be bent by hand and used in situations where awkward bends are unavoidable.

Similarly, set wastes and overflows in a thin bed of mastic and tighten lock nuts against a washer. Remove all surplus mastic. While fittings should be firmly tightened, avoid excess tightening, or you may crack the bowl or basin.

On a wash hand-basin fit a trap with a 75mm deep water seal. The seal is to prevent smells from filtering back from the soil system. The deep seal helps to prevent siphonage of the water by the pull exercised by other services connected to the soil waste system.

Screw the pedestal to the floor, using plastic or rubber washers and brass screws. Never tighten metal against chinaware, or it may crack.

Once the basic plumbing-in has been done, attach the basin to the pedestal. On many types, this sits on the top of the pedestal. Some may have securing wing nuts, also using a washer as a buffer against cracking.

A basin should be connected up as far as possible before hanging with taps, waste and overflow. Fit taps, waste and fittings then carefully line up the bracket with a spirit level.

It is important that fixings are firm. Drill a hole in the wall, the dimension of the screws, using a masonry drill, fit wall plugs and then screw the fitting to the surface On a plasterboard or studded wall, hang using gravity toggles or similar fixings. If the basin is not firmly anchored, it may come away and rupture connections, causing a flood.

Locate the basin to ensure that the fitting projects

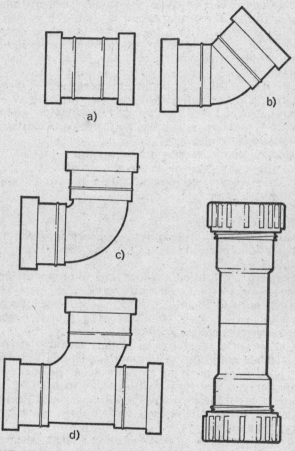

34. **Different Types of Waste Connector.**
   a) straight connector
   b) swept 135° bend connector
   c) 90° knuckle bend
   d) 92½° swept 'T'
   e) multi socket straight connector

through the centre hole of the bracket, then fit a washer and a flanged backnut over the waste. Tighten by hand then a further three quarters of a turn with a spanner. Tighten wingnuts, with a washer between these and the basin, then fix the basin firmly in place on its locating pins through the rear of the basin on to the bracket.

Overflow outlets may be incorporated into the body of the basin and automatically link up with the waste connection. If these do not, you will have to fit a combination waste and overflow, which has a flexible connector to join up to the waste outlet.

Modern plastic wastes utilise a rubber ring to complete the water seal once the capnut of the fitting is tightened. These must correspond in size with the connecting waste pipe.

Fitting a bath or bidet
Baths and bidets are similarly connected. Waste traps are available either as P or S traps, dependent on the installation.

Connect a bath using a 38mm trap and pipework and a basin or bidet with 32mm waste services. Where a 32mm pipe connects to 38mm pipework, use a swept branch tee connection. This may be either of a push-fit type, or joined using solvent weld cement.

Cut the tube squarely and slightly chamfer the edges to facilitate entry into the fitting. Apply a little washing-up liquid to the pipe end to lubricate it and make entry more positive, then push well home. A rubber ring forms a seal between the pipe and the fitting. Tighten the fitting capnut by hand, plus a final further three quarters of a turn with a spanner.

You can connect up sections using straight connectors, either solvent welded or with a locknut sealing washer. Fix waste pipe to walls securely with clips, maintaining a slight fall and avoiding dips in the pipe. Do not position pipe clips close to connections joining up sections of pipe, as this may inhibit longitudinal expansion and distort or dislodge the connection.

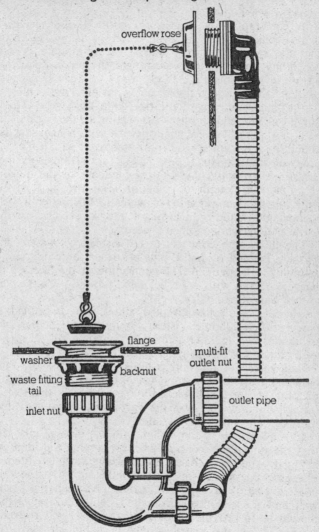

overflow rose

flange

washer

waste fitting
tail

backnut

multi-fit
outlet nut

outlet pipe

inlet nut

35. A Type of Bath Trap, incorporating an overflow.

Fitting a new toilet

You can replace a cast-iron high-level cistern with a lighter, plastic one. However, water is heavy, so ensure that the cistern is firmly fixed. A wall-mounted cistern has fixing holes for screws through the top portion. Use a spirit level to check it is level.

Other than close-coupled suites, cisterns are connected to the pan by means of plastic 38mm flush pipe. This is curved at one end to allow connection to the back of the pan. The pipe is easily cut to length with a hacksaw, but should be cut squarely and burrs removed with a file.

When cutting flush pipe, make sure that you have measured correctly, and that you adhere to the maker's recommended length of pipe or you may not have a sufficient head or pressure of water to flush effectively.

Pipes are made with a spigot and socket end, so that extra sections can be joined if need be.

The flush pipe connects to the cistern with a nut and washer. Tighten by hand, plus a further three quarters of a turn with a spanner. The connection at the back of the pan is covered with a rubber cone, slotted over the stem at the point of pan entry.

Siphonic and close-coupled suites are assembled by placing the siphonic cistern over the fitted pan and tightening two locking screws to tighten a rubber gasket around the joint and provide a seal.

Ball valves in flushing cisterns are fitted in the same way as in storage cisterns. Check that it is of the low-pressure variety, suitable for connection to the storage supply. Using a high-pressure valve means that replenishment of water takes a long time.

If you have to fit the siphon into the cistern, take care that the housing is centred when tightening the large nut fixing it. The dome or piston housing must be fitted on the same side as the ball valve. Make sure that the valve float and arm have good clearance between the cistern wall and internal mechanism and bend the arm slightly if need be to provide clearance and set the water level.

Connect to the water supply in a similar way to a storage cistern (see page 44). Use a swivel tap connector to fit a 15mm–22mm supply pipe. Overflow connection

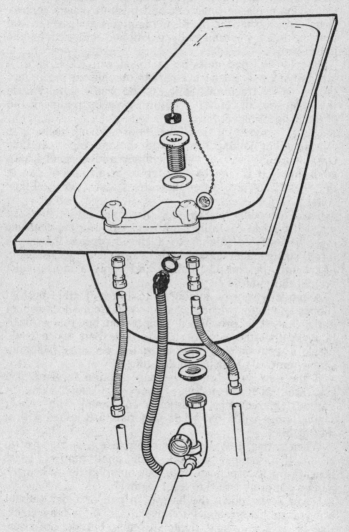

36. Typical Bath Connections.

is a similar arrangement to that of a storage cistern, using 22mm plastic pipework and push-fit plastic connections. Ensure that the overflow maintains a slight fall and that its outlet is prominently positioned and clear of the house wall.

An old WC pan must be removed with care, particularly where it is connected to vitreous glazed pipe, since this is easily fractured. Shut off the water supply, flush the toilet and disconnect the flush pipe by pulling it out of the flanged inlet at the rear.

Unscrew the pan from the floor. Where there is a mortar collar joining the trap to the soil pipe, carefully chip this away with a club hammer and a small, sharp cold chisel. It is sometimes safer to break an old pan at the bend to avoid undue stress on the soil-pipe collar.

Once the collar is exposed, place rag into it to keep out débris, then carefully chip away any mortar segments. An older way of jointing to a glazed pipe is to wrap a tarred string, called gaskin, tightly around the pan spiggot, insert into the soil-pipe collar, and apply a mortar fillet around the joint.

A modern way of joining is to use a flexible push-fit rubber connector which has a screw-in stem and a rubber outlet seal. This provides a perfect seal but retains flexibility so that there is no stress on the pan which could break a conventional mortar seal. This also facilitates simple removal of the pan at any time.

If the new suite brings the pan position forward, you can use extension pieces, either in plastic, china or vitreous, glazed pipe. Plastic is connected with rubber sealing rings while the other materials are joined with a mortar fillet.

When fitting a WC pan or bidet, use a spirit level to ensure that the pan is level. Slide small timber wedges beneath on a suspended floor but on solid floors bed the pan on a mortar screed to level them.

Never screw down the base of a pan or bidet without using a rubber grommet to insulate it, or it may crack. Use brass screws and tighten evenly, but do not over-tighten. Check finally that the fitting does not rock.

Toilet seats are easy to fit. Fixing is through pre-made holes in the back of the pan.

Soil System

In older homes, it is usual to find what is called a two-pipe soil system. Waste water from baths, basins and bidets feed into a hopper head then, usually, via a trapped yard gulley to the main drainage. Toilets are connected to a soil pipe, joined directly to the sewer drainage below ground.

The exceptions to the use of the single-pipe system (see Chapter 2) are certain ground-floor connections, such as a separate WC located on the other side of the home to the main soil service, and waste outlets from the kitchen.

All soil branch connections must be swept in the direction of flow. To avoid suction, no branch connection on the soil pipe should be closer than 200mm below the entry of a WC branch. All waste pipes should slope as gently as possible; to an extent, this is governed by the angles of fittings and connectors.

Modern soil systems are usually made of PVC or ABS pipe, using seal-ring joints which allow the pipe to expand. Because of the high rate of thermal expansion, clips and fittings must be carefully aligned to allow longitudinal movement.

9

SHOWERS

A shower in the home can go almost anywhere. It takes limited space, uses less water and is more pleasant than using a bath because it provides a continuous flow of clean water. Showers are also safer to use than baths. Older people, for example, have less risk of slipping when getting in and out of a shower.

You can provide a shower in a space of as little as 750mm × 750mm. Deep cupboards or recesses beneath stairs or space on landings are possible positions to site a shower—subject to your being able to provide supply and drainage.

A shower attachment attached to a bath-tap mixing set converts a bath into a shower, allowing water to be directed to the bath or to the shower head. A separate shower attachment can also be provided. You can fix a shower head with a flexible pipe to a wall clip so that water can be directed on to your head or at chest height when standing.

When using a standard mixing set, always adjust the flow to a comfortable temperature by opening the cold supply, then gradually adding the hot. For maximum safety, thermostatic mixing valves are best, for these exercise close control over temperature and are unaffected by any possible pressure variations, which could cause a dangerous increase in the flow of hot water. Non-thermostatic valves are similar in appearance and operation, though not free from problems of pressure variation.

Shower screens and curtains are the best choice for fitting round a bath to retain water splashes. A shower cubicle consists of three fixed sides, usually with a curtain on the fourth or an opening door.

It is best to give a shower, particularly a non-thermo-static one, first-pull call on the system to help maintain the most even temperatures possible; this is most readily achieved by plumbing in a separate supply from the cold cistern and ensuring that your hot-water supply arrangements give first call on the shower. Most mixing valves allow the spray force to be varied. Under no circumstances connect this type of shower directly to the mains.

You need a minimum water head of 900mm for successful satisfactory operation, though 1220mm to 1520mm gives a more effective spray. The head is the point taken from the base of the cistern to the top of the spray. An atomising spray, which produces a much finer shower of water than the standard rose spray, requires a minimum water head of 2450mm to work effectively.

A minimum bore of copper pipe of 15mm is needed in most circumstances. If bends or configurations in pipework layout are likely to reduce pressure, use 22mm bore tube. The shower should be connected to the low-pressure side of the domestic system, the cold-storage cistern. Before connecting up a shower to a plumbing system, first drain down existing pipes and interrupt the supply from the cold cistern.

Draining off the water in the crown of the cistern will be sufficient to shut down the flow of hot water but supply from the cistern must, of course, be shut off.

Connecting the shower follows standard plumbing connections. Connections on the shower head are usually compression ended.

Try to hide and disguise pipework by routing it in or behind a wall, allowing access to pipes via a false panel. If pipework is to show, it is advisable to use stainless-steel tube, which has an externally more attractive appearance than copper pipe, or paint the copper pipe to merge with wall surfaces. When boxing in pipework, many makes of shower allow connections to be made at the back of the fitment.

Upstairs it is sometimes difficult to obtain the head of water required without fitting an accelerator pump into the circuit. You can often overcome this by building a stout platform in the loft to raise the height of the cold cistern. This, of course, means that it will have to be drained down and pipework extended then reconnected.

Modern gas and electric shower units are often the answer when fitting a shower. These are compact and neatly styled and placed over the bath. Pipework supply simply consists of a cold supply, simplifying the operation of plumbing in. These showers work on an instantaneous basis in that they heat only the small quantity of water passing through them as it is demanded.

Gas-fired units have to be terminated on a flue to an outside wall.

10

WATER HEATERS

Until comparatively recently gas water heaters were seen in terms of the old fashioned, often cumbersome and frequently temperamental geysers. Today's gas water heaters are not only better looking but are also safer and more efficient in use.

Most types of gas heater have a balanced flue and must be fixed to an external wall to allow fresh air to be drawn into the appliance and the waste products of combustion to be vented out. Appliances with a balanced flue are room-sealed (meaning they do not take air from the room) and this eliminates the ventilation problems that existed with some types of older heaters.

There are five types of water heater available, with versatility enough to cover almost all possible hot-water requirements in the home.

An *instantaneous sink water heater* is normally fitted beside or above the kitchen sink and supplies hot water on demand through its own spout or the kitchen sink tap. The instantaneous heater has a fairly low output but will supply about 2.5 litres of water per minute.

For circumstances where the demand is higher and hot water is required at several points, such as bathroom, kitchen, wash hand-basin or shower, a *multipoint heater*, which is larger than a sink heater, may be fitted. This type of heater has sufficient output to supply several points. Multipoint heaters are also instantaneous in that they heat water only as it is demanded.

Dependent on the size of the heater, between 5 litres and 7.5 litres of hot water per minute can be supplied at any one tap. Siting is normally no problem as modern heaters take up no more space than the average size kitchen cupboard and they can be fitted in either the kitchen or bathroom.

Storage heaters provide a self-contained system consisting of a well-insulated tank, with a built-in gas burner. The tank will hold up to 100 litres and the water is thermostatically controlled. This system is ideal for homes where there is no satisfactory hot-water storage cylinder but where regular hot water is needed throughout the day.

A *circulator* is in effect a miniature gas boiler which is used in connection with a conventional storage cylinder. This can be sited in any convenient position, but if your airing cupboard is large enough could usefully be positioned beside the hot-water cylinder.

Circulators are thermostatically controlled to give a constant supply of domestic hot water. In some cases it may be possible to fit a special economy valve which can be set to heat the whole tank or alternatively just keep a few litres at the top permanently hot.

You may decide to use a *back-boiler* which fits behind a gas fire in an existing hearth. The boiler is concealed behind the fire so you retain an attractive visual focal point and at the same time heat hot water which is fed into the home's hot-water storage system and kept at a thermostatically controlled temperature.

Equally, you are able to have complete flexibility in use since the fire and boiler are independently controlled. This type of back-boiler should not be confused with a larger appliance which, sited in the same way, can be used to give partial or full central heating.

It is very important to have any type of water heater regularly serviced to ensure that these well used machines are kept in good working order. A yearly overhaul and clean up will pay dividends in efficiency, safety, reliability and fuel conservation.

11

ROUTINE PLUMBING MAINTENANCE
AND REPAIRS

A well-installed plumbing system will seldom give trouble. The most likely faults are dripping taps and overflows, problems which can be put right with the minimum of disruption to water supply in the home.

Taps
Taps come in for a great deal of use, so they are the most vulnerable part of the system. There are two main types of tap—the pillar tap, which has a vertical inlet and the bib tap, with a horizontal inlet.

On high-pressure mains, when the tap is turned off, a resilient washer presses down over the valve seat and prevents water from flowing from inlet to outlet. The washer sits loosely on the spindle base. The handle is attached to the spindle; when the handle is turned the spindle rises, allowing water pressure to lift the jumper so that water can flow. On a low-pressure supply, the jumper is attached to the spindle, since the pressure would not be great enough for the jumper to lift.

The washer is the weakest part of the system. This wears, or the valve seat becomes obstructed as a result of foreign bodies which prevent the washer from seating correctly, causing the tap to drip.

Before you dismantle a dripping tap, try turning it on fully, for a sudden force of water may dislodge a foreign body. Shut off water supply before you dismantle a tap to change a washer. This is not necessary, however, in the case of the "Supatap" type, the design of which automatically shuts off the water supply, leaving you access to the inside of the tap.

First remove the tap cover. If you have to use a wrench to loosen this, wrap a piece of cloth around the tap head to avoid marking or damaging the surface.

If the tap threads are clogged, clean with spirit, then lightly smear with petroleum jelly. Loosen the hexagonal nut on the headgear to expose the washer on the valve seat. The low-pressure pattern of a jumper is attached to and comes off with the spindle. Jumpers are made of brass, with the washer fixed to this with a brass nut. Sometimes, this assembly seizes up and distorts when you try to free it, so have a spare jumper and washer set to hand.

Grease the threads of the nut when attaching the new washer to provide ease of movement. Use the correct type of rubber washer for hot and cold taps, though synthetic washers are suitable for either. You can trim an over-sized washer to fit.

Where water bypasses the washer the valve seat may be pitted and worn and need regrinding, a specialist job. An alternative is a nylon washer and seat set which goes over the existing valve to do the same thing.

If water trickles over the tap cover top, a leak has probably developed through the gland. This means you have to remove the tap handle to gain access. Unscrew the small grub screw holding the handle to the spindle. If the handle is difficult to remove, use a piece of hard-wood between the handle and the cover as a wedge to help free it.

Loosen the gland screw and take out the old packing from the stuffing box and replace this with wool, cotton wool or string soaked in petroleum jelly, grease or tallow. Compress it into the stuffing box, leaving enough space so that the gland screw can be firmly tightened back. If you overpack the stuffing box, the tap will be difficult to turn.

Toilet cisterns

Modern toilet cisterns are piston actuated, while older types have a bell-type mechanism, easily identified by its belled central dome. Should a ball float become per-

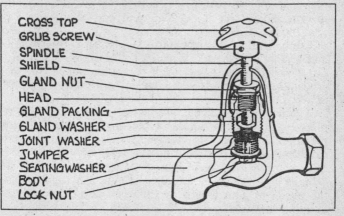

CROSS TOP
GRUB SCREW
SPINDLE
SHIELD
GLAND NUT
HEAD
GLAND PACKING
GLAND WASHER
JOINT WASHER
JUMPER
SEATING WASHER
BODY
LOCK NUT

37. Arrangement of a Domestic Tap.

forated or an outlet washer become faulty, cisterns may overflow.

The piston siphon works by forcing the water in the cistern above a disc or plunger and down the flush pipe, where a partial vacuum is created which siphons the water in the cistern. This disc is perforated, allowing water to flow through it, and is closed by a plastic flap or washer on the up stroke. This flap fulfills the purpose of a non-return valve and, if damaged, the flushing action may fail or be impaired.

To change a damaged washer, flush the cistern and tie up the ball arm so that the cistern cannot refill. Bail out any excess water, then unlock the nut beneath the cistern securing the flush pipe to the siphon.

The flush-lever linkage needs lifting out to get access to the siphon, so that you can remove the plunger disc from the bottom of the dome. Remove the small retaining washer holding the valve washer in place and replace with another of the same size. If you do not have a replacement, you can make one by cutting a disc of heavy PVC, using the washer as a template.

Replace any worn washer between the siphon and flush

pipe and apply a smear of non-toxic plumbing compound to consolidate the joint. The unit can then simply be reassembled.

The ball-valve arrangement is similar on both a flushing and a storage cistern. This may not operate satisfactorily for a variety of reasons, such as a perforated ball float, eroded valve seatings, lime deposits, grit on moving parts or a worn washer.

If you have to change the valve, ensure that it is replaced with one of similar type—high, medium or low pressure. A faulty valve washer is easily replaced by removing the split pin securing the lever of the piston. In some cases, you have to remove a cap on the end of the cylinder by undoing a washer retaining cap which allows the piston to detach into two halves, so you have access to fit the new washer.

Flush out any grit behind the valve seating before replacing the valve.

A new ball float screws on to the threaded spindle on the float arm. You can temporarily repair a perforated ball by tying up the float arm, unscrewing the ball and draining it then encasing it in a polythene bag, tying the neck of the bag over the lever arm.

A faulty valve washer, causing a continuous overflow, may be as a result of worn metal valve seatings. This can be reground but can be replaced with a nylon seat capping. If the seating is cracked, it cannot be repaired and must be replaced. New valves are usually fitted with nylon seating pieces.

Periodically check the stopcock. This should not be left fully turned on, or it may stick and be difficult to shut down quickly in an emergency. Turn the stopcock on then close it slightly. Grease the stem of the tap from time to time with petroleum jelly to keep it free.

Air locks may occur after you refill following attention to the system. Usually, this is because a body of air is trapped between two volumes of water in a pipe—often when there is a change of direction from up to down. Mains pressure may not be sufficient to force the entrapped air bubble to the nearest tap or valve.

One way to clear this is to join the high-pressure to the

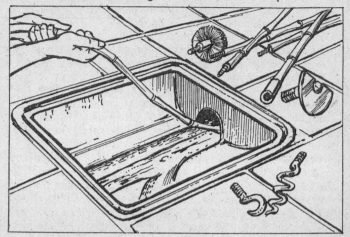

38. An Inspection Chamber.
Together with a set of rods and various attachments.

low-pressure side by linking the appropriate taps with a
section of hose. Leave a tap open on the blocked side to
vent the entrapped air, and turn on both taps.

If the airlock is on the hot-water side, block off the
vent pipe above the cold cistern before following the
same procedure, remembering to unblock the vent once
you have cleared the airlock.

Where you experience frequent air locks, see if the routing of pipes is in any way tortuous and liable to cause the
problem. Sometimes you may have to fit an air-release
valve fitting at a point of persistent air blockage to vent
this. This can be either a manual or a more expensive
automatic type.

Blockages
Frequent inspection helps potential blockages from occur-
ring then getting out of hand. The trap or water seal on a
bath, sink or basin is intended to give you access by
removing a plug on the side of the trap or unscrewing a
base, so that débris and water can be released. Always

have a large bucket to hand in these circumstances to collect the unpleasant waste residue.

If a WC pan becomes blocked, you may be able to free it by careful use of a rubber plunger. Too much stress, however, could break the pan and cause a major disaster!

Manholes or inspection chambers enable you to gain access at points of entry or outflow, where blockage may occur. In new soil-drainage systems, permission can be granted in many instances to provide a rodding-eye terminal, or RET, which enables you to rod an obstruction clear.

One of the main causes of blockage is a roughed surface or fractures to the walls of the access chamber, or the benching, the surround to the drainage channel, which may be too shallow or not smooth enough. This should slope gently on either side of the channel. Clean off débris and repair, bond the surface with a dilute PVA solution, such as woodworking adhesive, then make good with a 1:3 mixture of cement and sharp sand, applied with a steel float. Take care to keep mortar out of the gulley. Allow this to set before the section is in use again.

Modern inspection chambers are available in a moulded plastic and seldom give problems once installed. If the lid of the manhole is broken, buy a new rim, for these are sold as a matched pair and should be a close fit. Mortar in the new rim and liberally apply a heavy grease to the inside of the rim before putting on the lid. If the lid is removed, it is advisable to remove old grease and replace with fresh, free from foreign matter, which could get into the manhole and may cause a blockage.

Drain rods are a useful acquisition—in case they are ever needed. You can, however, hire these. Rods are made in short sections which screw together and are fairly flexible. There are a variety of attachments. The main ones are a rubber plunger, hook, scraper, corkscrew head and brush. The corkscrew is for lifting plugs in manholes but is also useful for removing débris.

If there are several manholes in the drainage chain, start nearest the home until you find an empty manhole. The blockage is between that and the next back.

Fit a piece of chicken wire rolled into a ball over the

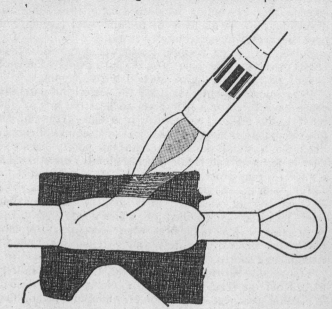

39. Preparing a Leaded Joint.
It is neatly finished by heating the plumber's metal to a plastic
state and wiping the joint with the moleskin dipped in tallow.
The piece of sprung metal on the right facilitates handling.

outflow of the empty chamber, making sure that it cannot
get into the pipe and be difficult to remove. This allows
water to flow but stops solid matter.

The rubber plunger is the best tool for clearing blockages. Screw this on to the end of the rod and insert into
the chamber, turning the rods in a clockwise direction so
that they cannot unscrew. Use the hook if the blockage
proves persistent, and the scraper to remove adhering
débris. Once the blockage is clear, thoroughly flush out
the length of drain with a hose and use the brush to
clean off encaked débris which could cause further
blockage.

Burst pipes usually occur on leaded pipework in unlagged lofts. Prevention is always better than cure, so always lag pipes with foam or mineral-wool lagging, but never old rags, which encourage vermin.

Bursts are caused because frozen water expands, then bursts or distends the pipe. You do not normally know of a burst pipe until it thaws out and starts dripping.

If you detect a burst, shut off the water and carefully use a blow torch or a hair dryer to heat the area of the burst. Catch released water in a receptacle. You can cut out a damaged area of pipe and join in a section of copper pipe. On a small burst, you can tap gently back the damaged section and repair it using plumber's metal. This is a joint-wiping process.

To cut in a new section of pipe in leaded pipework or to repair a joint, you need to be able to wipe a simple joint. This is a highly skilled job, which needs a great deal of practice, so it is often best, where possible, to replace old leaded pipework entirely, but a repair may still be essential as a short-term measure.

You need a blowtorch, a hardwood cone or metal dolly to bell out the pipe, and a mole cloth, to wipe a leaded joint. You also need tinning solder, plumber's metal, flux, tallow and plumber's black.

Cut and trim the pipe using a hacksaw. The mouth of the cut tube then has to be enlarged or belled. You can do this by tapping in the hardwood cone, twisting it between blows or insert the dolly into the mouth of the pipe and rotate outwards to enlarge the mouth. Bell the pipe out to a depth of around 40mm.

Paint plumber's black around the pipe at about 50mm back to stop solder from spreading beyond the joint limits. A completed joint is about 75mm long.

Insert a cleaned and prepared end of copper tube into the joint. Clean inside and outside the tube with a penknife or shavehook until the metal is bright. Clean the tube with fine wire wool and bevel the end slightly to facilitate entry into the leadwork. Similarly apply plumber's black on the tube.

Coat mating surfaces evenly with flux, heat the solder and bring the two ends together, keeping a moving even flame, and apply solder neatly around the joint. Heat the plumber's metal carefully to a plastic state only, so that it does not run, until it fills the joint up to the rim of the belled portion.

Warm the moleskin in the flame and dip it in tallow. Reheat the solder, and wipe the moleskin around the joint, using a sweeping circular motion. Build up the joint, alternatively applying plumber's metal and wiping with the heated moleskin and tallow. Build up the metal over the body of the joint and neatly feather the edges. Allow the joint to cool thoroughly before manipulating it in any way.

12

ABOUT CENTRAL HEATING

Central heating is no longer the luxury it was once considered to be. Even so, many homes still lack this amenity.

There is nothing new about central heating. The Romans introduced it to Britain over 2,000 years ago. The well-appointed Roman villa had underfloor ducted wood-fired heating, kept fired by teams of slaves. Such is the march of progress that the modern 'slave' is a compact boiler, doing all the work with limited attention.

Many homes are well below basic standards of insulation, so that heating is costly and comfort levels often poor. Many other homes rely on a limited form of central heating, using older, solid fuel boilers serving two or three radiators. The number of well-insulated homes and well-designed and installed central-heating systems is even smaller.

The UK is essentially cold for much of the year—it is not surprising, for it is on a latitude as far north as Labrador, so space heating makes sense.

Initially, you should look to the standards of thermal insulation of your home, for there is no sense in allowing precious heat to escape to the atmosphere. The loft is a major area of loss and this ideally should be insulated with 75mm–100mm of glass-fibre mat or similar insulation.

Look around doors and windows and fit proprietary insulating strip.

Cold air can be drawn in beneath outside doors, so consider fitting a threshold bar where needed. Sometimes, gaps occur between walls and door or window frames;

fill these with a proprietary mastic—this can be bought in a dispenser 'gun', rather like icing cake!

Designing then installing your own system is not unduly complex but does, of course, require careful planning and care and attention. It is possible to buy all the equipment you need from a specialist heating supplier, many of whom offer advisory services and can provide design and layout and also give useful discounts.

Your choice of fuel is the first consideration, followed by the type of system you want. (See Chapter 13, page 93). For many, gas is a natural choice, but this is not available everywhere, although you can settle for a Calor gas tank, which is recharged periodically. This is located outside and well clear of the home.

For general structural reasons, you normally have to select a 'wet' heating system—one where heated water is circulated around pipework from the boiler to radiators or other heat-emitting surfaces. Ducted, warm-air systems are not easy to fit in homes once built.

Two-pipe small-bore systems, with separate flow-and-return pipework, are the most widely installed, but there is a better case for microbore systems, using smaller pipe still, or a single-pipe loop system, ideal for skirting convectors, which give a comfortable even heat output.

One-pipe systems are now seldom installed using conventional radiators, for the water circulates in turn to radiators and becomes increasingly colder as heat is exchanged. This means that the last radiators on the chain have to be somewhat progressively larger to achieve the same heat output. Smallbore and microbore systems use individual flow and return pipes, so that the heat emitted is constant from each radiator.

Once you have chosen your fuel, the position for the boiler should be selected. Large, free-standing boilers have a very common position—in the kitchen. Many boilers now, however, are compact and can be fixed to walls, stowed beneath cupboards and located in the loft, the garage or even on outside walls, liberating much-needed kitchen space.

You can preserve the open-fire vista with a room heater, of which there are various types, not all able to provide

full-house central heating. In this case, you have to augment the heating with supplementary heating, such as gas
or open fires, or use a zone system, which heats each part
of the home in turn. This, at best, provides background
heating. Gas fires with back boiler are another choice.

After you have decided on your type of heating system,
plan the layout, avoiding, where possible, very long runs
of pipework, for this helps to produce imbalance between
radiators. Some radiators may get hotter and 'raid' heat
from others. A smallbore system will usually require
balancing—that is the lockshield valves on one end of
the radiators may have to be adjusted to equalise the
output across the system. Microbore and loop systems
(described later) are largely self-balancing.

Once you have ordered your 'kit of parts', check carefully that you have everything and are not going to be
held up during a weekend, for example, for a vital component. Buy or hire the tools you need, and, when buying,
choose the best you can afford. Those required for plumbing work will largely cover your needs for central heating.

13

COMFORT LEVELS
AND CHOICE OF FUEL

In these days of rising costs, fuel, like almost every commodity, is expensive. There is no such thing as cheap
heating fuel as all forms of heating are relatively
expensive.

Often the choice of system is secondary to the choice
of fuel. Basically the choice lies between gas, oil or solid
fuel, either used to fire a complete system or as a combination— for example solid fuel part central heating, backed
up by electric or gas fires which either supplement heat
requirements in the coldest weather or can be used for
the occasional cold evening in high summer.

Solid fuel
Solid fuel provides the cheapest heating, followed by oil
or gas. However, you need to provide storage for the fuel
and accept the inconvenience of certain refuelling and
the removal of ash and clinker from the appliance.

Solid fuel can be divided into two main types. These
are natural fuels taken as mined, cleaned, graded for size
and sold and processed natural fuels, which may be
carbonised or briquetted. With the exception of house
coal and some types of briquette all solid fuels can be
burnt in Smoke Control Areas.

House coal, which gives off some smoke in burning,
anthracite and Welsh dry steam coal, which are smokeless
are natural fuels.

You can burn house coal on open fires, including combination grates and openable room heaters. Welsh dry

steam coal and anthracite are suitable for open-room heaters.

A high-output room heater capable of providing full house heating has a secondary combustion chamber which literally 'gobbles' the smoke produced and this type of appliance widens the type of fuel that can be burnt while still conforming with the Clean Air Act requirements.

A conventional open fire will not be suitable for serving a full central-heating system. If you want to retain a room fire, you might choose an open fire with a high-output back boiler, or if this consideration is not important a room heater with a high-output boiler. The other choices are an independent domestic hot-water boiler without a thermostat or one that is thermostatically controlled.

If you choose an open-fire with high-output boiler it will heat the room where it is sited, feed between two to five average radiators and a towel rail and supply domestic hot water. This type of system may be zone-controlled in larger homes, so that you can choose, with controls, to heat a section of the home or 'zone' at a time.

On a room heater with a back boiler, direct heat is distributed into the room via a grill at the top of the fire.

Room heaters are generally kept burning throughout the winter and need replenishing between two and three times in 24 hours.

There are three types of solid-fuel boiler—the cast-iron boiler, called the section boiler—which consists of a number of sections bolted together. These are normally hand-fed. More sophisticated, and hopper fed is the gravity feed unit which has a steel boiler.

Gravity-feed boilers are usually thermostatically controlled. An electric fan which gives a heat intense enough to melt the ash into clinker which is easily removed, works in conjunction with the boiler. Heat utilisation efficiency is high—between 70–80 per cent on most boilers and even higher on some.

The third type of solid-fuel boiler is the pot-type. This has a circular or square fire box, and is also thermostatically controlled. The boiler is made of cast iron or steel. You can expect heat-utilisation efficiency of be-

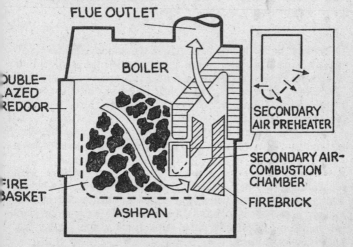

FLUE OUTLET

BOILER

DOUBLE-
GLAZED
FIREDOOR

SECONDARY
AIR PREHEATER

FIRE
BASKET

SECONDARY AIR-
COMBUSTION
CHAMBER

FIREBRICK

ASHPAN

40. A Smoke Gobbler, (Radiation Ltd.)

tween 60 and 70 per cent. You can use a pot-type boiler
without a thermostat to heat a number of radiators but
the boiler will need more attention than one thermostatically controlled.

Heat emitting surfaces such as steel-panelled radiators,
slim line skirting radiators or fan convectors can be used
with solid-fuel heating boilers.

Oil
There are three main types of oil-fired central heating
boiler; the wallflame, the pressure jet and the vapourising
boiler. Traditionally boilers tend to be sited in the kitchen
—standard pressure-jet boilers are noisy and best sited
outside the home in a boiler house. Down-firing pressure-
jet boilers, however, are quieter in operation and can be
installed indoors.

If you are using oil-fired central heating you will also
need a sufficiently sized oil-storage tank accessible for
delivery and correctly positioned. Additional requirements
such as preparing the site for the tank, buying the tank

and laying the supply line to the house tend to make oil-fired systems more expensive to install.

Gas

Once you have decided to install gas central-heating you must ensure that the mains supply is adequate. If this is not so the Gas Board will lay a new supply line.

In some rural areas, gas is not laid on, and the cost of bringing in a main would be prohibitive. Here, you may have to use oil or Calor-gas.

With gas boiler installations you can choose between conventional-flue boilers or room-sealed units vented by a balanced flue.

If you want your gas-fired boiler to function with maximum efficiency, especially if you choose a low-water content boiler, you will also need a sophisticated control system. Low-water content boilers have a very high level of operating efficiency, heat up quickly and have fast heat-recovery times.

14

HOW A HEATING SYSTEM WORKS

In most cases, a plumbed-in or 'wet' system provides the best arrangement for domestic central heating.

Wet systems circulate heated water from a boiler to radiators or convectors around the home, via small pipes, then back to the boiler for reheating. A pump or circulator aids water distribution. This is called 'forced circulation.'

Smallbore systems
Many modern systems use smallbore pipework. There are two basic types of small-bore system—the single pipe and the two-pipe system. The two-pipe system, with separate flow and return pipes, is the most usual of the small-bore systems.

Two-pipe systems are more efficient than single-pipe systems. An exception to this is the single-pipe loop system which you can install with natural (i.e. without a fan) convectors.

Microbore systems
Microbore is an extension of the two-pipe smallbore system. It uses a pipework of only 6mm, 8mm, 10mm, or 12mm, fed from central distributors, called manifolds, compared with the small-bore system which uses pipes of 15mm and 22mm and, sometimes, 28mm.

Both types of system circulate pump-assisted hot water along pipes, to provide central heating, and, usually, domestic hot water. Because of the smaller bore of microbore pipework, there is a lesser volume of water to heat and distribute and, given the advantages of fast heat up and heat recovery, lower costs. Microbore can, like smallbore systems, be gas, solid fuel or oil-fired.

Other microbore advantages include low heat loss from the run of pipework, far less fabric dislocation during installation, simpler and faster installation, plus the use of far fewer heating fittings than a smallbore system. It is important to use a special high-recovery hot-water cylinder or a microbore heating element in a 'direct' cylinder.

Apart from the expense, fittings are a possible source of leaks and take time to fit. Microbore also provides virtual freedom from air locks and is virtually self-balancing. Balancing is making adjustments to the flow volume to various parts of the system, so that radiators or convectors are at correct heat.

Manifolds possess separate flow-and-return compartments. They are best mounted as centrally as possible—in a conventional two-storey home, you would usually locate one beneath the upstairs floorboards and a second below ground-floor floorboards.

If a home has a solid floor, or is a bungalow, a drop-pipe system can supply ground-floor radiators and convectors. The very small pipes are not obtrusive and can also be neatly boxed in.

Microbore heating can be used in either an open or a sealed system. Sealed systems are intended to operate at higher temperatures than open systems, which work at the conventional smallbore temperatures. Conventional steel-panelled radiators are unsuitable for higher-temperature sealed systems.

For microbore use, it is best to use a high-recovery cylinder. This has an inner coil of high efficiency which heats the water quickly.

A microbore element can be inserted into the immersion-heater boss of a direct cylinder. A direct cylinder is one that does not contain a heating element. The fitting of a microbore heating coil, however, effectively converts the cylinder to an indirect one, where heating and draw-off waters do not co-mingle.

This element also gives the cylinder high-recovery properties, though slightly below those of a high-recovery cylinder. Connect supply using 10mm pipework and threaded fittings.

Generally, the greater the number of radiators required, the cheaper a microbore system is to install, compared with a smallbore system. The design and layout of the home, the routing chosen or imposed for the pipework by this, boiler position and disposition of radiators all play a part in determining the most realistic layout.

Good microbore design is a combination of radial and smallbore layout without the same concern of possible airlocks of the former. The size of the house in no ways prohibits or inhibits the use of microbore.

Sealed systems

One curious misconception is that a sealed system, because in operation it is slightly pressurised, is in some way 'dangerous'. In fact, a smallbore system could potentially be more dangerous. If, for example, on a 'conventional' open system, the gas valve sticks in the open position and the valve in the header cistern in the closed position, the boiler will eventually boil off all the water unless there is a high-temperature limiting device, independent of the other boiler controls, causing potential vast damage to the appliance and the home.

The sealed system eliminates the need for an open 'header' cistern at high level, together with the ancillary ballvalve pipework and fittings. With a bungalow, for example, the problem of low static head can cause water to be pumped over the vent pipe or air to be drawn in. In sealed systems, an automatic air vent is used. Most operate on a float principle which rely on the tendency of air to rise above water and trip off a mechanism which vents the air. The problems you can face with an open system include water noises and air locks. Air is a retarding factor so far as heat transfer is concerned. Its absence in a sealed system increases the efficiency of heat transfer between water and the appliance.

On open systems the feed-and-expansion cistern absorbs the expansion of the heated water and maintains a constant pressure within the system, dictated by the height and in consequence the static head of the system, and provides a source of replenishment for water lost from evaporation.

One of the advantages of higher temperatures is that smaller heat-emitting appliances can be used, saving both space and cost. This latter, smaller type of boiler is faster in recovery response with greater flexibility in use.

Boilers for microbore

Ideally, a microbore system should use a low water-content central-heating boiler. These use heat exchangers of copper or stainless steel which retain little residual heat, so that system controls react fast and accurately to actual circuit temperatures. Older, cast-iron boilers are called 'high-thermal boilers', while small, low water-content units are called 'low thermal-content boilers'.

High-thermal boilers have advantages where continuous heating is required at a constant temperature. The 'wild' heat given off by a cast-iron boiler is often enough to heat a kitchen without a radiator. Conversely, the heat emitted by a low water-content boiler can be disregarded.

When sizing a system using pumped-primary circulation for domestic water heating, you can disregard the usual calculations of 2.93kW/h (10,000 Btu/h) usually allowed for hot-water heating in a gravity hot-water system.

Water in the system is merely the medium used to transfer heat from the boiler to the radiators. The lower the water content, the faster the system will heat. While a cast-iron boiler of higher thermal content takes longer to heat up, than to cool down, the smaller water quantity in a microbore system and a low water-content boiler provides a more accurate temperature control over the system.

Radiators and heating appliances

You can choose between conventional, steel-panelled radiators, skirting and fan convectors and thermal-type radiators, the latter much superior in performance to conventional radiators.

A disadvantage of steel-panelled radiators is that they are a localised heat-emitting source, so cold and even

draughty areas can occur between them. This disadvantage
does not occur with fan convectors, for they push out
heat which circulates all around the area.

Skirting convectors—sometimes called linear heaters—
have many qualities lacking in panel radiators. A low-
level, even emission of heat provides an even, wrap-
round level of comfort, and you do not experience the
'hot-head-cold-feet' syndrome, common with steel-
panelled radiators. Finrad is a leading make.

Temperature is kept above 'dew point', which helps to
prevent condensation without drying out the air, with all
the consequential discomfort and potential damage to
furniture and fabric this can produce.

These convectors are produced in varying lengths and
consist of aluminium-finned copper tube of 15mm or
22mm diameter, housed in a shallow wood-topped case
with a white, stove-enamelled steel front panel. A
damper provides control over the heat output.

Skirting convectors project about 50mm from the wall
and are only 250mm high.

Brackets, holding the panels into which the element
fits, are simply screwed to the wall. Fitting does not
necessitate removal of skirting boards of standard height.

The sections of finned tube are joined using either
capillary or compression fittings, and then the front panel
is simply snapped on.

When the damper is fully closed, only about 20 per
cent of full heat is emitted, enabling you to control your
comfort levels. The closed position is ideal for maintaining a trickle of background heat, to keep the fabric and
mass warm in an unoccupied room.

The loop system is a principle of a continuous loop of
pipe of 15mm or 22mm tube connecting the skirting convectors. A larger system is best served with 22mm convectors and joining pipework.

An advantage of the loop system is that it cuts down
disturbance to the fabric of the home—you can take tube
through walls and merely use dummy cases to cover it,
presenting a continuous line of panelling.

Upright natural convectors (without fans) are also
available and can be ideal for small areas, such as kitchens

or bathrooms, where it is not possible to fit a run of skirting convector.

A fan convector consists of heat-exchange pipework with a fan to accelerate the exchange and flow of heat. The fan is adjustable but in a correctly sized system can be left at its lowest speed, generating an even, slightly accelerated flow of heat. A thermostatic control is incorporated so that the temperature level at which the fan cuts off can be chosen.

An advantage of fan convectors is that you can use a convector in place of several radiators. Although these are basically more expensive than steel radiators, the reduction in pipework, and the greater efficiency and economy will quickly recover an initial extra outlay.

15

SIZING THE HEATING SYSTEM

Since even a degree or two over your heating needs adds materially to bills, the system should be correctly 'sized'. That is the heat output in any room should be exactly that needed to maintain the required temperature level.

Apart from heat loss through various materials, it is necessary to ensure that air is changed to remove stale and moisture-laden air. The loft should be insulated, gaps should be eliminated around windows and doors. Chapter 19 on Thermal Insulation (page 134) deals with this fully.

The usual comfort levels and air changes per hour are:

Kitchen	16°C	1.5–2
Toilet, hall, cloakroom, staircase, bathroom	19°C	2
Living room, dining room	22°C	2
Bedroom	15°C	1.5–2

Heating systems are sized in kilowatts (kW/h) or Btu/h (British thermal units per hour). One kW equals 3412 Btu/h. The metric kilowatt is the preferred value.

For homes requiring 14.6kW/h (50,000 Btu/h) of heat, a four-litre capacity pressure vessel is needed. Between 14.6kW/h 29.3kW/h (100,000 Btu/h), a 7.5-litre vessel is used, and over 35kW/h (119,420Btu/h), a 12-litre vessel is required.

A small house may need less than 13.9kW/h (45,000 Btu/h) an hour, while a larger detached or 'semi' may need 17.58kW/h (60,000Btu/h) or more. A four-bed-roomed home may need up to 29.3kW/h to cope with really cold weather.

The working temperature of a standard or low-temperature open system is 82°C. For sealed systems, elevated temperatures between 82°C and 99°C are often used.

When working out your heat requirements, take note of the future use of bedrooms as bed-sitting rooms. In the latter case, allow for a temperature of 22°C.

Ignore conduction of heat between rooms. These temperatures are related to the outside or ambient temperature of 0°C at freezing point.

Despite the need to conserve heat, there will be losses through small chinks in the fabric of the home, usually providing the necessary air changes per hour. This is essential if the atmosphere is to be fresh, clean and free from stuffiness.

While there is a detailed mathematical formula you can use to find exact heat requirements, in fact this simple rule-of-thumb method is quite accurate in average conditions. This is to measure the room volume in cubic metres, and for a temperature of 21°C, multiply the desired volume by 65.

To obtain a temperature of 16°C multiply by 54 and for 13°C by 39, to provide, in every case, the figure in watts. To arrive at the kW/h rating, divide the figure by 1000.

For normal installation using radiators, the water content of a system is about 30 litres for every kilowatt of heat and around 15 litres per kW for skirting or fan convectors.

Return water in a microbore heating system cools by about 11°C for effective heat utilisation. This is called the 'temperature difference'.

The amount of radiator surface needed can be arrived at from data supplied by the makers. Skirting convectors

emit roughly 470W at a temperature of 82°C and 540W
at 96°C per metre run.

A rule-of-thumb method of determining heat output is
to allow 2.60m² of radiator surface for every 28.30m³ of
space for a room of average volume. Allow 3.15m² for
double radiators on low-temperature systems.

Boiler

A boiler should possess a higher output than the total
capacity required. Allow about 25 per cent extra for
exceptionally cold weather, when the boiler works hard.
However, the high thermal efficiency of low water-content
boilers means that a small boiler will heat to the same
level as a larger, cast-iron-jacketed boiler.

Controls

To work well and with the best economy, you need a
number of controls on the system. These are in two types,
primary or system controls, and secondary, or comfort
controls. The former are used directly with the boiler;
the latter to sense room and ambient temperatures. This
is all explained in Chapter 16 (page 107).

Radiator sizes

It is relatively simple to establish the size of steel-
panelled radiators you will require, if this is your choice,
by manufacturers' ratings. From charts, which a heating
supplier can offer, you can work out the amount of radiator area in relation to the output of your system.

Radiators are made in all shapes and sizes and can also
be supplied curved or angled to go round areas such as
window bays. Where space is at a premium, it is possible
to fit double radiators. These, however, give out 20 per
cent less heat than two single radiators. A triple radiator
is 32 per cent cooler still.

Fan convectors are adjustable but should be sized on
average room heat requirements when the convector is
at its lowest running speed. You can adjust the speed of
the fan, thus increasing the output. There is a wide range
of convectors of this type, providing a full spectrum
of outputs.

In calculating the amount of skirting radiator required, when fitting these on a loop system, add 10 per cent to the length of the downstream room element and deduct the same amount from an upstream room where two or more rooms come together on a loop. This allows for the gradual reduction in water temperature around the loop.

You can also accommodate a second element inside a skirting convector to give an increased heat output—around 30 per cent higher. However, it is important that you use a high enough volume of water to ensure a balanced water flow and even heat output—22mm diameter supply is usually needed.

For full precision when calculating your heating needs, a useful investment is the Mear 5B Domestic Heating Calculator. With this, you merely set two dials to read off your heating requirements, together with sizes of pipework and equipment. The calculator, made of thick Perspex, also provides answers for insulated walls and roofs and indicates necessary allowances for double glazing. It only costs a few pounds, from M. H. Mear and Co, 56, Nettleton Road, Dalton, Huddersfield HD5 9BT, Yorks.

16

UNDER CONTROL !

One degree over—far too small to be detected physically —can put 5p in the £ on to your heating bills and can add up to a fair sum over the year.

Without the use of controls your temperature error from comfort norms could be considerable, adding greatly to your heating costs.

Heating controls can save a great deal of money for room temperatures and the temperature of domestic hot water can be closely controlled by thermostatic devices.

There are two basic types of heating controls—primary controls, providing a combustion safeguard and usually fitted to the boiler during manufacture—and secondary controls, to control the output of heat to provide the best levels of comfort, together with the lowest operating costs.

Primary controls
Certain primary controls, such as automatic air vents, pressure and temperature gauges used with pressure vessels, overheat thermostats and automatic shut-down valves are controls you may add to a sealed or pressurised heating system.

Secondary controls
Secondary controls range from cylinder thermostats, either of the automatic or mechanical type, to motorised valves and three-port diverter valves, controlling the flow of circulating hot water to the cylinder and the heating system. Other secondary controls are programmers and a variety of time clocks, both simple and sophisticated thermo-

static radiator valves, room thermostats and frost-sensing thermostats, the latter mounted out of doors.

Mechanical controls

The most basic controls are the valves fitted to radiators, the handwheel and lockshield. The former provides local control to shut down a radiator, partially or fully, and the lockshield control is adjusted during commission of the system to adjust the flow of water to balance the output of the radiator, so that it operates efficiently. These controls when shut down, allow removal of a radiator for maintenance and painting.

It is possible to fit mechanical controls to shut down the supply to the cylinder, if you prefer this method to wiring up basic electrical circuits.

A mechanical control consists of a bellows-type thermostat, inserted into the immersion-heater boss of the cylinder, which shuts off at the desired temperature, simply adjusted on the body of the thermostat, to shut down the supply of hot water. This type of control can be used with a gravity type of hot-water system but never where heating is by an open fire lacking thermostatic control.

Electrical controls

Though controls usually operate at mains voltage, some modern room thermostats operate on a low voltage and merely plug into a small control box fitted on or near the boiler. Low-voltage controls are claimed to work to even finer limits of thermostatic tolerance, saving further money.

A relay box is sometimes required to co-ordinate the various controls, such as a room thermostat, boiler thermostat, and controls such as the programmer, motorised valves and cylinder thermostat.

The most usual system of controls uses a programmer, generally coupled with a room thermostat, or thermostatic radiator valves, to control the temperatures inside the home.

A programmer allows you a choice of timed hot water alone or hot water with heating, and you can set a time-switch to operate to your needs over a 24-hour period. Some sophisticated programmers allow for a choice of nine programmes or more.

Diverter and motorised valves

Unless you use a pumped-primary system, which requires diverter valves or motorised valves, you cannot have heating without domestic hot water.

The diverter valve is a three-port motorised valve fitted to the flow outlet from the boiler by compression connectors, serving the heating and the hot-water pipework.

The valve swings to either side to provide heating or hot water. Some of these give 'priority' either to heating or to hot water, so that the 'priority' circuit is always kept at an optimum temperature before swinging back to supply the other part of the circuit. Another type shares the flow between the two systems, compensating evenly any temperature loss.

Diverter valves are wired in conjunction with the cylinder and room thermostats to the boiler to control the desired temperatures.

Two-port motorised valves fit directly into the heating and the domestic hot-water pipes using compression fittings, and are also wired back to the boiler and the room thermostat or programmer. These open and close the valve to control the flow of water as needed.

Thermostats

One type of room thermostat dispenses with a programmer and works on a 'set-back' principle. With this, the system never actually shuts down. At a pre-determined time at night the system cuts back to a 'trickle' temperature, which you also predetermine, and resumes full operation next morning. This means that the fabric and the space in the home never grow completely cold, so less heat is needed to top up lost levels in the morning.

The set-back setting can, however, be overridden. The system is used with a conventional cylinder thermostat to provide constant hot water. This type of system is claimed to give lower heating costs than programmed systems which shut down completely at chosen times.

A room thermostat should be located at about 1.5m above the ground, clear of direct heat or draughts and not in a room of main occupation. This is because the heat radiated by a group of people would artificially affect the overall temperatures.

For whole-house control using a single thermostat, the heating system should be accurately sized (see Chapter 15, page 103), so that when the temperature is correct in one room it provides accurate comfort levels in all others.

Thermostats fitted to hot-water cylinders clip around the body of the cylinder. These are best located at a position of about one-third of the way up from the bottom of the cylinder. The temperature is shown in a dial, which you adjust with a screwdriver. Generally, this is best set at 49°C.

Individual radiators or convectors can be controlled by an in-line valve, with a key-way to control the water, so that these can be shut down partially or fully.

Controls which restrict the gravity circulation from non-thermostatic solid-fuel appliances, where the pipework acts as a 'heat leak' should not be fitted.

A few sensible rules should be followed with electricity. Never connect wires up with the mains switched on and always follow the wiring circuits very carefully indeed. If in doubt, inquire! Help can be provided by manufacturers or suppliers of products, or you can consult a qualified electrician.

Wiring in the electrical circuits is not particularly complicated, using standard 1mm^2 cable. Manufacturers provide full details and simple point-to-point wiring information to enable you to do this successfully.

Finally, where carrying out the wiring yourself, check carefully all the connections before switching on and testing. You can adjust the boiler, cylinder and room thermostat controls manually to check the firing operation of the boiler and the function of controls such as the motorised or three-port diverter valves.

17

INSTALLING YOUR HEATING SYSTEM

Always work to a plan.
Assemble all the materials and fittings needed in advance.
This is a suggested outline:

- Plan the pipe runs to ensure the minimum dislocation.

- Lift floorboards, and put them back loosely so that
you can work quickly.

- Fit all radiators and connectors.

- Connect up radiator pipework and put in manifolds
where these are to be used, and 'header' pipework.

- Instal, where required, the expansion cistern and its
related parts.

- Fit the hot-water cylinder and pipework for the
domestic hot-water supply.

- Instal the boiler and any flue pipe.

- Fit the gas supply or oil line. as supply can generally
be taken from a branch fitting on the outlet side of the
meter in small bore tube. First, check with the Board
that the supply is adequate to meet the needs of the
system.

- Connect up the primary circuit between the boiler
and the hot-water cylinder.

- Join the pipework circuitry to the boiler.

- Fill the system, with the pump isolating valves shut down, and check for leaks.

- Flush out at least twice.

- Fit the pump into circuit. The isolating valves on each side enable you to remove it at any time without draining down the circuit.

- Wire in all thermostats and other electrical equipment. Switch on the circuit. If any part of the system is running 'cold', some other part may be 'raiding' the heat. In that case, you will have to fit an in-line control valve which enables you to restrict water flow and balance the system.

- After the system has been running for about two weeks, flush it again.

- Check for leaks before finally fixing down floorboards and then top up lost water levels.

Techniques used to instal central heating follow those for domestic plumbing. Pursue a methodical approach, working in stages and checking connections as you proceed. Prepare rooms in advance, moving furniture out or away from work areas, and lift and loosely replace floorboards. Do not leave them raised, for this could cause an accident.

Running the pipework
When running pipework, take account of the lines of the joists. If you *have* to run pipework at right angles to the joists, either drill these so that the pipework can be located about 50mm deep, or notch the joists to recess the pipe without friction. Allow sufficient clearance for thermal expansion, to avoid friction noises and stress as pipes expand and contract. Drill the holes a little larger than the tube. Make sure that drilled holes or notches are in line so that this imposes no stress on the pipework. Take care when fixing back boards that you do not puncture the tubing.
Where tube goes through wall surfaces, fit sleeving a

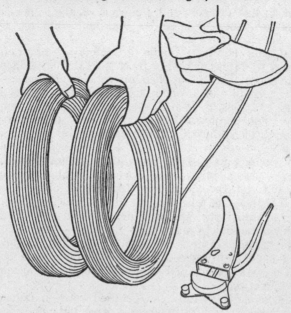

41. Running out the Microbore Pipework.
  Also showing a hand bending unit.

little larger than the tube to allow for free movement.
Never mortar or plaster a pipe going through a wall.

Ensure that main pipework, where this runs parallel
with joists, is supported at intervals with pipe clips. Tube
in an exposed position, such as beneath downstairs floorboards, should be lagged, to prevent unnecessary loss of
heat and to minimise the chance of freezing if the system
is switched off during cold weather.

Microbore tubing
Microbore tube, however, does not usually need to be
lagged, for the water content is very low. Where microbore tubing is exposed to view, it can be painted over to
blend with the wall. These small tubes can also be
plastered into a wall surface without problem, though it

is best to have access—and a concealed tube is at risk if fixings are made with screws and nails into the wall surface at any time.

You can, however, obtain a variety of proprietary ductings to cover microbore pipes on external surfaces.

Microbore tube is supplied on reels of 20 metres or more in length and in 6mm, 8mm, 10mm, or 12mm diameters, and consists of malleable, soft-drawn hard-temper copper. You simply roll out the pipework, cut the amount you need, then connect up with capillary or compression fittings.

Microbore pipe can be cut with a hacksaw. Do not, however, use a pipe cutter, for this slightly burrs the ends and restricts water flow. Microbore tube is easily bent by hand—but take care not to kink it when doing so. You can also bend pipe with a hand-held pipe bender, which you can buy or hire.

The distance from a manifold to a radiator or convector should not exceed 7.5 metres with a total combined flow-and-return pipework to the outlet of not more than 15 metres.

In general, 8mm tube can be used between radiators and manifolds. However, where a large radiator or convector is some distance from the manifold it may function better using 10mm diameter tube, while a small unit, fairly close to the manifold, may be connected with 6mm tubing.

Draincocks
Always fit a draincock at the lowest point in the system, so that you can drain it down easily. This fitting has a small key-way (MT) tap.

Where pipework runs below floorboards, fit the draincock at the lowest point. If pipe is 'dropped' (from above) in the case of a solid floor, fit the pipework runs along the skirting, and fit the draincock in the pipe run or near a connection to a radiator.

Safety valve in pressure systems
A safety valve should be fitted to the system sized to its pressure, rated in 'bar'. The safety valve is usually set at 2.3–5 bar. This operates only if the circuit overheats, such as when there is a loss of water pressure.

Microbore manifolds

The heart of a microbore system is really the manifold, a connector which distributes the microbore tube to radiators. The manifold, in turn, is linked by flow-and-return 'header' pipework to the boiler, usually of 22mm diameter, though you can use 15mm on a small heating system. Large systems may need 28mm header pipework.

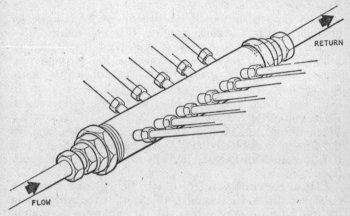

42. A Manifold.

Microbore heating systems ideally utilise a radial layout. If the manifold is centrally placed, this ensures a high degree of self-balancing so that there is seldom any need to adjust individual flows to radiators.

Connections at manifolds are usually of 10mm diameter and compression-ended. A small reducing set is needed where either 6mm or 8mm tube is connected. In most cases, tube of 8mm diameter is sufficient to provide the comfort levels needed. You can use more than one manifold, each served by flow-and-return 'header' pipework from the boiler.

When making connections to manifolds, curve the tube to a shallow bend so that the water flow is as smooth as possible. This will ensure a better system performance, with an even pressure of water to all parts.

Support the fitted manifolds so that they do not place undue stress on all connecting pipework.

On a microbore system, it is not strictly necessary to provide individual radiator valves, but these can perform the functions of isolating valves, so that you can at any time shut down the valves and remove the radiator for maintenance, cleaning or painting behind.

Smallbore

A microbore or a smallbore system are both basically two-pipe systems—using separate flow-and-return pipes to radiators. If you prefer a smallbore installation, it follows a similar installation technique, though your running costs may be greater than that of a microbore system.

Fixing radiators

When fitting radiators to walls, ensure that you achieve the firmest possible fixings. A full radiator is heavy and if it becomes dislodged, the effect can be a disastrous flood!

Use a heavy-duty screw of the length and diameter recommended by the supplier of the radiator when fixing the radiator brackets. Line up the brackets accurately with a spirit level, so that the radiator is not tilted when lifted on to the brackets.

Never try to fix into plaster surfaces but always firmly into the wall. First, drill a hole of the correct diameter, with a masonry twist bit, then screw the bracket into place, using a proprietary wall plug.

Studded or plasterboard walls need special care and very heavy radiators cannot effectively be hung. Lighter radiators can be fitted using a proprietary cavity fixing.

There is a range of these. If possible, try to screw-fix directly into a stud, at least at one point. The studding framework provides the timber support for the cladding plasterboard.

Radiators are usually best hung beneath windows, since these are traditionally cold areas. The effect of glass is to cool warmed air, which contracts and produces draughts. Window areas are also places where furniture, which can

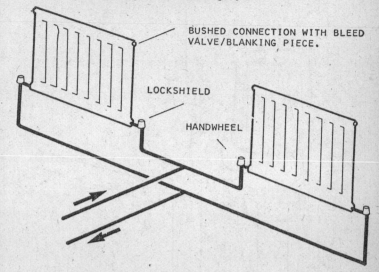

BUSHED CONNECTION WITH BLEED VALVE/BLANKING PIECE.

LOCKSHIELD

HANDWHEEL

43. A Two Pipe System.
  Schematic diagram showing two radiators on a pipe run. Bleed
  valve can be fitted to either end. Valves and lockshields will
  normally require reduced bushes to fit to radiator.

impede heat flow, is not traditionally positioned. However,
where it is not possible to position a radiator beneath a
window, fix the radiator to an outside wall.

Radiator valve fittings
Air vents should be fitted to all radiators, with a blanking
connector (stop end) on the opposed side. Radiators are
made to accept valves and pipework on either side at top
or at bottom. It is usually neater to fit the valves at the
lower position and blank the top on one side, and fit an
air vent on the other side. You can fit either straight or
angled radiator valves, to meet the pipework arrangements.

All fittings—valves, vents and blanking connections—
are threaded and require PTFE tape around the threads
to effect a sound water seal. Make connections for vents

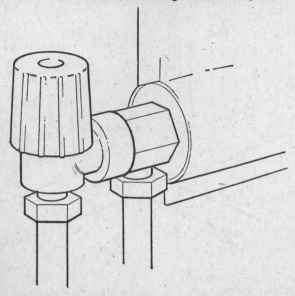

44. Special Twin Entry Radiator Valve.
This is used for Microbore.

and blanking piece and bushes before hanging the radiators.

You will generally need to fit a reducing bush to a radiator to accept a radiator valve—a handwheel, to provide individual control and a lockshield, for balancing purposes.

There are also special twin radiator valves developed for microbore which neatly take in the connecting tube at one end.

Loop systems
Fitting a loop system as an alternative to microbore or smallbore follows a similar work practice. You can have one or more loops, dependent on home layout. Like microbore, loop systems are ideal with low water-content systems. Place an air vent in the highest point of each loop

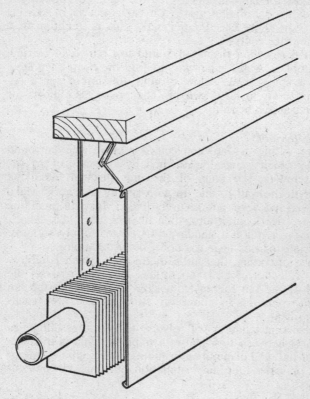

45. A Skirting Convector.
The damper at the top can be opened to control the temperature flow. (Finrad Limited)

and, of course, a draincock at the lowest point in the
circuit. As a rough guide, allow about seven kW/h
(25,000Btu/h) for each loop.

Each loop should be controlled by a balancing valve,
to adjust for imbalance between the circuits. Though you
do not need isolating valves on each section of skirting
convector, some Gas Boards make this a condition of a
maintenance contract.

When screwing the bracket and top panels of skirting
radiators to walls, take care to line these up accurately
with a spirit level. Allow around 100mm of space beneath for air to be drawn in. This space also allows for
cleaning access beneath.

Fan convectors

Before fitting a fan convector, remove the surround
casing, which is usually attached by a couple of screws,
and screw-fix the body of the unit through the fixing
points to the wall to line up with supply pipework. Make
sure that it is level and securely fixed. Make all plumbing
and electrical connections, then fit back the outer case.

The fan requires a standard 13A power supply, so make
provision for this near the point of installation.

Once operating, the unit's thermostat, which is adjustable, will control basic operation. You can also set the
speed of the fan to run from slow to fast. With the fan
not in operation, a convector still yields a low, background heat.

Correct installation will give a temperature difference
of 11°C between flow-and-return pipes. This is irrespec-
tive of the type of pumped installation—smallbore, microbore, or series loop, an installation utilising skirting convectors.

Sealed systems

With sealed systems, higher working temperatures can be
achieved without risk of boiling. A sealed system should
incorporate an automatic air vent, since some air is
initially retained in the circuit, which has to 'boil out'.

Live water always contains a high volume of air. This
eventually reaches the highest point in the circuit and is

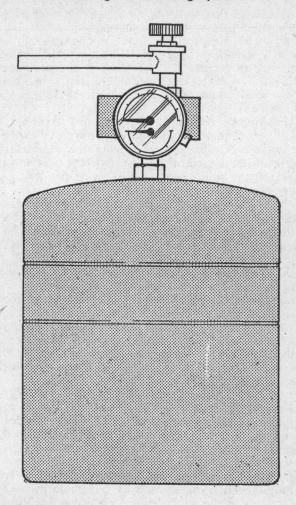

46. A Pressure Vessel.
  · The top indicator shows pressure and the lower indicator shows
  temperature. (Microbore Merchants Ltd.)

then vented, leaving 'dead' water which will neither corrode nor form lime scale inside the pipework.

A high-limit thermostat should be connected to the boiler in a sealed heating system to shut down the system in the event of failure of any control. A pressure-release valve, which operates mechanically if the temperature rises above a certain point, is also desirable. These may come fitted as standard.

A diaphragm pressure vessel containing a rubber or plastic diaphragm, filled with air or nitrogen, allows the water in the system to 'flex' on expansion. It can be fitted anywhere in the system, but is usually most conveniently located near the boiler, connected to the heating flow pipe via a tee-piece connector.

A useful provision is a temperature and pressure gauge —usually of the combined type—so that you can check that the pressure is correct and there are no leaks, indicated by a fall in pressure. These are often incorporated with the pressure vessel, as illustrated.

Such a pressure vessel can be supplied by any good heating stockist. Pressure of water in the system is sized in atmospheres, a normal system operation is at about 2.5A (atmospheres). The vessel should be sized to be at least half an atmosphere below the setting of the pressure-release safety valve, which should always be incorporated into the circuit. A pressure vessel takes up about 1/20th of the water content, or 5 per cent of the water content of the system.

Gas connections

Before installing a gas-fired system, first check with the gas authority that your main supply is adequate. It might be necessary for them to run a new service with a larger-bore supply pipe and, possibly change the meter.

Making gas connections on the boiler is really a basic plumbing operation, but consult the gas authority on the supply of gas to the appliance and connection to the gas meter.

It is permissible to provide the gas supply from the meter using copper tube—usually 15mm–22mm—but some authorities may run a supply in iron barrel pipe which is rather more clumsy and needs stocks and dies to cut threads if you choose to do it yourself.

Fitting the boiler
When fitting a wall-mounted boiler, ensure that the fixings are secure. Establish accurate levels by lining up the fixing positions with a spirit level. Fit basic connections to the boiler before hanging it. It may be necessary to have assistance to support the boiler when fixing it in place.

With a room-sealed boiler you will also have to cut an opening for the sealed-entry duct. Make sure that this lines up accurately with the position of the boiler.

Pipework connections to the boiler, usually located on the same side of the boiler, are the flow (top) and the return beneath. Connect up and take out pipework from the boiler with the minimum of angles to ensure better flow characteristics.

The boiler connections take threaded fittings. On such fittings, wind PTFE tape around the threads to effect the water seal. These are usually female-threaded (Fl). Connections on boilers and cylinders are able to accept larger-bore pipework and generally have to be reduced by using reducing fittings or bushes, adaptors which enable the smaller-pipe pipework connections to be made.

The pump
A high-head pump (circulator) is required for satisfactory water circulation and can be adjusted over a range of pump speeds, representing the 'head' or pressure of water or resistance of the system.

The size of the pump depends on the capacity of the circuit. Manufacturers' data makes it straightforward to choose a suitable pump. A high-head pump has a water head adjustable between 1.5 metres and 4.8 metres, so you have a fair amount of latitude in a given pump.

The pump should connect into the flow pipe and never in the very lowest part of the system, for this encourages the collection of sediment. It should be installed with the blades and face in the vertical plane.

The pump has threaded connections, requiring the use

of PTFE tape, and an isolating gate valve should be fitted on each side to allow the pump to be removed at any time without having to drain down the entire circuit. Support the pump by pipe clips to its connecting pipework.

The expansion pipe

Fit an expansion pipe to a feed-and-expansion cistern in an open system. This can be inserted, using a tee-piece connector, before the pump. A feed-and-expansion or 'header' cistern is a small, cold-storage cistern, usually made of PVC or GRP (glass-reinforced plastics, or glass fibre).

On a pumped-primary system, where the heating pump or circulator pump circulates hot water to the hot-water cylinder, there is no need to locate the cylinder higher than the boiler, which is necessary on a gravity hot-water system. This allows a wider choice of boiler and hot-water cylinder location.

Before filling the system with water, ensure that all joints and connections are readily accessible in the event of leaks.

Many water authorities oppose direct connection to the mains for filling. Supply has to be connected to the low-pressure or storage supply and at a low point, allowing air to rise and subsequently vent. A non-return valve, such as a stopcock, must be incorporated in the supply line to prevent the reversal of contents during heat up and pressurisation.

Either connect a hose via the cold-storage supply to a fill point in the system—this can be a stopcock connected via a tee-piece connector—or if you connect directly to a supply, fit a stopcock and open it to fill the system slowly.

Some Water Authorities may insist heating systems should not be fed directly from the mains, but via a make-up bottle, mounted above the boiler.

Open all air vents to expel air as the system fills. Monitor this closely and as water starts to trickle out shut down each vent with the vent key.

On an open system, as the system cools and water contracts, air rises to the highest point, usually an upstairs radiator. The presence of air is indicated by the fact that the radiator will grow partially or fully cold, indicating the presence of entrapped air. This is vented by opening the air vent with the vent key (also called a bleed key), to release entrapped air which will come out under pressure. Venting is complete when water is released. You may have to repeat this procedure several times over a number of days. Eventually there will be no live water in the system, which reduces the possibility of corrosion.

Sometimes an air lock will persist but will usually clear within a few days during normal system operation. If it persists, check for blockages or tortuous pipework causing air to remain entrapped.

Corrosion and leaks

It is advisable to pour a quantity of a proprietary corrosion inhibitor into the system once you are satisfied with its operation and are unlikely to need to drain it down.

Once the system is installed, check each connection carefully for leaks before replacing floorboards. It is a good idea, in fact, to fit boards back loosely for the first week or so, for small leaks can develop initially as pipes expand and contract if fittings are not properly tightened.

If a fitting leaks, it is a simple matter to tighten a compression connection. A leaking capillary joint cannot be resoldered with water in the system, for this cools the pipe as you heat it. It is necessary, at least, to drain down that particular leg of the circuit.

However, there is a proprietary liquid sealant you can buy from a good stockist which you can pour into the circuit. Use only the quantity recommended for the water content of the system. This will seal leaks.

Before finally filling, it is desirable to flush out the system to remove any residual sludge. On cast-iron boilers, there is usually a residue of casting sand in the jacket which needs to be flushed out. Flushing is more effective if done at mains pressure.

Once a sealed system is free of air, the pressure should remain even. Any loss of pressure, shown on the dial of the pressure gauge, should be investigated, for it probably indicates a leak.

Similarly, if you continually have to replenish water in
an open system, this also indicates a loss. For this
reason, only refix flooring temporarily, but safely, until
you are sure that there is no loss of system water.

Once the system is operating effectively, the expansion
vessel, on the sealed system, and vent pipe, on an open
system, will take care of system water expansion.

Regular maintenance
On an open system, check from time to time that the
header cistern ball valve mechanism is operating, since
fresh water is introduced via this cistern to compensate
for a small amount of evaporation loss. Very occasionally,
you may have to vent a higher radiator to remove collected air.

Flues and flue linings
Never connect a conventional-flued boiler to an unlined
chimney, for the corrosive effects of gas waste, and,
to a lesser degree, oil will eat through the brickwork in
time.

Flue lining can be done using a stainless-steel flexible
liner. You can use other linings, such as sections of
asbestos-cement pipe joined together with fireclay cement,
or vitreous-enamelled pipe, the latter usually used to connect the boiler to other flue-lining materials.

For the average small boiler, 100mm–125mm diameter
pipe can be used to connect the flue. Flue sizes can be as
large as 200mm diameter.

Calculate the needs accurately, allowing for the bends in
most chimneys, so that you do not have too much waste
but are not short. If, however, you have too little lining,
you can join sections together with a special collar, or fit
the lining in a section of vitreous enamel or asbestos pipe
at the room end.

Stainless-steel linings must never be used with solid-
fuel appliances, for some fuels produce hydrochloric or
sulphuric acids which attack the liner.

Before fitting a flexible metal flue liner, first sweep the
chimney, then chip away the flaunching mortar around the
chimney pot so that you can remove it. When working on

a roof, take great care and only use firmly supported access ladders.

The lining is best fed down the chimney from the top. A wooden nose cone is usually provided. This has a pull string attached to it to facilitate pulling it through. Check that there are no projections which can damage or impede the lining of the chimney.

Excess tube lining is easily cut off with a hacksaw, but cut it carefully, so that the strands of the lining do not unravel.

At the boiler, clamp the lining clamps over the socket outlet on the boiler. At the chimney top, it is clamped to a fixing plate, to which you fit a shrouded cowl, before putting back the chimney pot and remaking the chimney flaunching, preferably with high-alumina cement.

With floor-standing boilers, an initial section of vitreous or asbestos pipe, angled to fit neatly into the flue opening, looks neat and enables an access panel to be fitted so that any build up of condensate can be drained.

Flues for room-sealed boilers
On room-sealed boilers, the procedure is simply to cut a hole through the wall and mortar the flue ducting into this, then bolt the flue casing to the outside.

Central-heating appliances are broadly classified as Class I or Class II. A Class I appliance is one run on solid fuel or oil and not exceeding 45kW in output. A class II appliance is a gas appliance not exceeding 45kW output. The flue from a Class I appliance must not be closer than 2.3m horizontally and at least 1m above windows. The flue of a Class II appliance must not be closer than 600mm horizontally to a window. There are special rules for balanced flues; usually these should not be closer than 300mm to an opening window.

Regulations concerning appliances are dealt with in parts L to M of the Building Regulations. The requirements for a given appliance will be stated in the supplied fitting instructions.

Flue outlets are sealed with asbestos string and fireclay cement on the outlet terminals of both floor and wall-hung boilers.

Non-combustible hearths and shields

Before fitting the flue, ensure that a floor-mounted boiler is based on a non-combustible hearth at least 15mm thick and extending 125mm beyond the back and sides, unless otherwise stipulated by the manufacturer. For wall-mounted boilers there should be a shield of non-combustible material such as a brick wall at least 25mm thick, with surrounding air space of at least 75mm.

Oil tanks and oil supply

An oil tank can be fitted in a convenient place in the garden. Choose one with a capacity of not less than 3,000 litres, to ensure an adequate capacity and the best price when buying heating oil.

Oil lines are usually connected up using manipulative fittings—compression fittings which you have to bell out to connect—with 10mm tubing. Tubing can be buried deep enough to protect it from damage.

Siting should be above ground in the open. Try to choose an unobtrusive setting or one that can be screened by trees or shrubs. It is possible to site tanks within buildings such as garages but in these cases you must comply with local authority regulations.

Good, substantial support is required for the tank. This may be brick pillars or steel frame. The latter is considered more satisfactory particularly when initially positioning the tank. If you build brick pier supports, the tops of these must be separated from the tank base by a waterproof membrane.

The first job is to measure out, clear and level the site. Next lay a 150mm concrete base on well-packed hardcore. The base should extend length and widthwise beyond the tank by at least 100mm.

Connection to the boiler is by means of an oil line. This can be in flexible copper or black steel and should be encased in a bituminous compound to prevent corrosion. A minimum diameter of 6mm is necessary for lengths up to 9 metres, and over this up to about 18–20 metres a maximum 10mm diameter tube should be used.

The supply line should run either below or above ground—as directly as possible to the tank and should

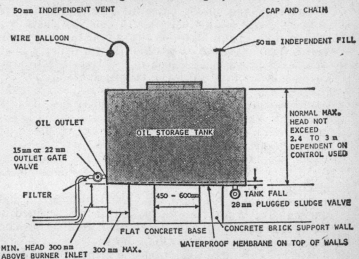

50 mm INDEPENDENT VENT

CAP AND CHAIN

WIRE BALLOON

50 mm INDEPENDENT FILL

OIL OUTLET

OIL STORAGE TANK

NORMAL MAX.
HEAD NOT
EXCEED
2.4 TO 3 m
DEPENDENT ON
CONTROL USED

15 mm or 22 mm
OUTLET GATE
VALVE

FILTER

TANK FALL
28 mm PLUGGED SLUDGE VALVE

450 - 600mm

FLAT CONCRETE BASE

CONCRETE BRICK SUPPORT WALL

MIN. HEAD 300 mm
ABOVE BURNER INLET

300 mm MAX.

WATERPROOF MEMBRANE ON TOP OF WALLS

47. The Oil Tank.
Showing some connection fitments.

contain a filter. If the line is buried make sure it is deep
enough to avoid damage from garden tools.

Oil lines are usually connected with manipulative fittings on copper pipe and with a petroleum jointing compound on black-steel threaded joints.

A burner's pressure depends on the difference between
the level of the burner, the height of the tank and the level
of the oil. The outlet from the tank must not be less than
300mm and the top of the tank not more than 3 metres
above the level of the burner.

A sensing element should be fitted above the boiler
burner to operate a fire-safety valve which should be positioned accessibly in the pipe line. You should also fit a
tee-piece connector in the line so that you can fit a flow-
rate gauge.

A draw-off valve can be fitted either directly to the tank
or close to it in the oil feed line. When fitting it to the
tank, position it about 50mm from the base to prevent
intake of sediment.

E

You require a fill or offset fill pipe, a 50mm vent isolating valve, a drain valve and a contents gauge.

Extend the 50mm fill to the edge of the tank and position accessibly for easy connection to the delivery hose. Terminate the pipe in a 50mm male-threaded (Ml) hose-coupling connection with a non-ferrous screw-on cap.

Where the tank is positioned at a distance from the roadway, you will have to provide an *off-set* line in black steel. This is normally 38mm–40mm diameter and is terminated with a 50mm male connection. On lines over 24 metres long, use a 50mm diameter tube.

You should also connect a valve, suitable for use with fuel oil, to prevent spillage when the hose connection is made up or broken.

An isolating valve, also with gland packing or diaphragm suitable for use with fuel oil, should be fitted in the tank outlet. This must be in an accessible position for connecting the oil supply to the burner.

A short vent pipe, taken from the highest point of the tank, capped with a wire-mesh balloon, must be fitted. This should vent into the open air.

To remove sludge and condensed water which may collect at the bottom you will need a drain valve which should be positioned on the lowest part of the tank.

Fix the contents gauge on the side of the tank. There are differing types of gauge but the simplest is one fixed right down the side of the tank, called a sight-level tube. Reading the level is simply done in the same way as you read a thermometer.

18

HUMIDIFICATION

While efficient heating and good thermal insulation may create a warm home, all too often the environment becomes less than comfortable because the air is too dry. Natural moisture is dried out of the air and results in a stuffy atmosphere which is not only unpleasant in that it can cause headaches, dry throats and eye irritation, but may also damage furniture and soft-furnishings.

A difference of 2° to 6° between the temperature at floor and head level can lead to a feeling of stuffiness and result in the attendant discomfort.

Physiological tests have shown that any surrounding requires four balancing factors to provide a comfortable environment. These factors are the ambient air temperature, the temperature of walls, furniture and so on, the relative humidity and the number of air changes.

To maintain comfortable temperature conditions the ambient temperature has to be increased to correspond with any fall in the ambient relative humidity. By increasing and balancing the moisture content in the air, the temperature can be lowered by several degrees, unnoticed by the human body.

Warm air can hold several times more water vapour than cold air; in fact air at 21°C holds 4 times more moisture than at freezing point (0°C).

In effect by heating our homes in winter we create

'thirsty air' which will extract the moisture it needs from the surrounding surfaces, furniture, soft furnishings, plants and us.

Air humidity is measured as relative humidity (rH). Relative humidity is defined as the percentage of water vapour in the air by weight at any given temperature to the weight of water vapour required to saturate the air at the same temperature.

This is shown as follows:

Temperature (°C) _rH%_   _Humidity_
About one litre

Temperature (°C)	rH%	Humidity
0	100	very high
15	50	medium (correct)
21	25	very low

If the rH factor is too low, we experience discomfort; too high it may result in a 'hot-greenhouse' situation.

Although people vary as to the degree of comfort they find acceptable, a level of 50 per cent (rH) in a room heated to 21°C is an acceptable situation.

A simple, yet uncomfortable way to redress the balance in over-dry rooms is to open windows, but this is not only wasteful in energy terms; it also creates unwelcome draughts.

The positive solution is to install some method of humidification which allows you to attain satisfactory comfort levels of moisture in the air and, at the same time, maintain an even temperature.

Humidifiers, of which there are many types, are basically water containers which allow the water to evaporate into the atmosphere and replace the moisture loss in the air.

One of the commonest types of humidifier is a hang-on-radiator humidifier. These may be made either of plastic or metal with perforated fronts and open backed. They are normally clip-fixed along the top or hung by clips on the front or back of the radiator. A large evaporative pad is stood in the filled water container. This absorbs the water which evaporates into the air as the radiator heats up. The hotter the radiator, the quicker the water will evaporate.

The maximum output from a 5-litre radiator humidifier is roughly 850ml per day. As a general rule, use as large a humidifier as possible. There are no maintenance costs but the pads should be changed at least once a year as dissolved solids in the water are deposited on the pads and, in time, render them ineffective.

Radiator-hung humidifiers provide preventative humidification but to restore the equilibrium of moisture content and achieve full comfort levels, additional humidification units may be necessary.

Fan-operated electrical humidifiers are free-standing and can be positioned anywhere in the home. Position them where the air can circulate freely. These also have a water container and either one or more evaporating pads or cotton wicks. The pads or wicks soak up the moisture and air is blown over them by an electrically operated fan.

Again, pads or wicks should be changed about every three months as they become clogged with dissolved solids from the water and dust particles in the air. Running costs are low. A unit running for 24 hours a day will consume about the same amount of electricity as a one-bar electric fire consumes in one hour. Fan-operated humidifiers are silent in operation.

Another type of humidifier is an atomisation unit. Water, converted into micro-atomised particles, combines with the dry air as it is drawn through the humidifier. This water/air mixture is ejected by a fast-spinning disc first through a specially designed and calibrated range of holes, then through the top aperture and into the air.

These units can be located anywhere in the home, running costs are low and the only maintenance needed is cleaning and topping up the reservoir of water.

Atomised units are high-output humidifiers and in normal situations do not need to run continuously but should be switched on for one to two hours twice a day.

While lower-output humidifiers such as radiator hung units, will keep the humidity in your home at a 'safe' level for both you and the contents, in an excessively dry atmosphere you will need a high-output humidifier.

A simple hygrometer-thermometer will give you both

room temperature and relative humidity readings. It is also possible to buy humidistats, which operate like thermostats, to control some types of electrically operated humidifiers, automatically.

19

THERMAL INSULATION

As modern heating, whichever type of fuel you use, is expensive, it makes sense to ensure that your home is as well insulated thermally as possible.

Heat loss can occur through the roof, walls, windows and doors, via chimneys and other flues and through the floor. It has been estimated that, in an uninsulated home, for every £1 you spend on heating only 25p actually goes to keep you warm. Not only will good thermal insulation help to keep fuel costs down, it will also keep your home more comfortable. Most heat loss occurs through roof, wall and floor areas so it makes sense to tackle those first.

All materials used in the structure of your home can be measured in terms of thermal efficiency which is known as the U value, or thermal transmittance co-efficient.

The 'U' value represents the amount of heat loss from one side of the structure to another, per m², per hour and per degree difference on each side. This is expressed as the formula 'U'=w/m² (watts per square metre) °C. The lower the 'U' value of a material the higher its insulant properties.

Roof insulation
Heat loss through the roof can represent the waste of up to 20p of every £1 you spend on heating wasted so represents an area that should have priority attention.

Basically there are two ways to insulate a roof area and which you choose depends on whether the area is used as living space or merely used for storage.

In roof living areas foil-backed insulated felt or bitumen backed paper can be fixed between the rafters. This will insulate and help to keep the loft area clean. For a greater degree of insulation semi-rigid slabs of insulating material may be fixed between the rafters.

If the roof is used purely for storage, you can insulate between the joists. Various materials, from glass-fibre matting, mineral wool, granulated polystyrene, felted wool or vegetable fibre, eel-grass to slabs of compressed cork can be used.

Where the joists are evenly spaced, one of the easiest insulant materials to use is glass fibre matting. This is easily cut with household scissors but you should wear gloves as particles of glass fibre may irritate the skin.

You can lay the matting, which is available in various lengths, over or between the joists but make sure that it is at least 25mm wider than the space between the joists. Drape the matting some way over the ends of the joists to prevent draughts creeping underneath.

As an alternative, loose-fill material—expanded polystyrene, cork, vermiculite, mineral wool—available in particle or pellet form, can be laid between the joists to a depth of at least 50mm—with full central heating 75–100mm.

Pour the material between the joists and rake over the surface to level it. You can use a timber template cut to fit over the joist to determine the depth of the filling. Tamp the material down firmly but do not compress it too hard. Loose-fill works on the 'string-vest' or cellular blanket principle—warm air is entrapped between the particles.

Seal the ends of the joists with building paper (bitumenised) but leave air bricks free. Air circulation is essential in a loft area and will not affect the loose fill which is quite stable, once laid.

Cold-water storage cisterns must be lagged. You can buy lagging sets consisting of polystyrene, mineral wool or compressed insulant board panels which fit round the cistern.

Alternatively, a simple cistern case may be constructed from chipboard on a timber frame. Make the frame larger than the cistern by 50mm–70mm and fill this gap with loose-fill insulant material.

Remember to leave out any loft insulation immediately

under the cistern, for a slow trickle of heat rising will
help to prevent the water from freezing.

Equally, once the roof area is insulated from the rising
heat it will become a cold area. This means that all pipes
must be lagged. You can use pipe-lagging sleeves which
wrap round the pipe rather like a bandage. Make sure
you overlap the joins and that entry points to the cistern
are protected. Secure at intervals with tape or string.

Pipe lagging may be rigid or flexible. The former may
be of glass-fibre, cork, expanded polystyrene or mineral
wool, while flexible materials available include foamed
polyurethane, expanded polystyrene or synthetic rubber.

Wall insulation
Most walls are constructed in one of three ways: solid
bricks or stone, cavity, that is one brick outer leaf and an
inner leaf of brick or building block, or an outer brick
or stone leaf with an inner 'dry' lining of plasterboard,
or building board. The latter is the type of construction
found in timber-frame houses and in modern frames in-
cludes a 'sandwich' filling of insulant material.

Solid walls can only be insulated by adding an inner
surface that will cut heat loss and raise the surface temperature, an aid in fighting condensation.

You might use polystyrene in sheet or tile form, insulating board, aluminium foil-backed paper or wood cladding.

Sheet polystyrene, a 2mm wafer thin 'paper', can be
cut with scissors and hung with a special heavy-duty wall-
covering adhesive. This material does, however, need
care in handling as it dents easily. Butt joint each piece of
sheet polystyrene or aluminium foil-backed paper to the
next.

Polystyrene tiles either plain or in a range of special
surface effects can be used on walls and ceilings. Select a
self-extinguishing, fire-resistant type and apply adhesive
over the entire backing before fixing. Do not dot-fix—
this is a fire hazard. While on safety—always paint with a
water-based paint—never gloss—again a fire hazard.

Insulating boards consist of a layer of polystyrene or
polyurethane sandwiched between various materials. Some

types are aluminium foil-backed and useful where there may be damp. Never fix to a chronically damp area to mask the trouble but after treatment aluminium foil-backed board may be an added precaution.

Wood cladding, panel or boards, in a range of colours and grains, makes a decorative 'warm' surface finish, with the added bonus that wood is a good insulant. On sound, level walls, panels may be adhesive-fixed or fixed on to a timber batten framework. To aid insulation, you can fix a 'skin' of mineral wall quilting behind the battens. When insulating any solid walls select the most exposed ones in your home first.

Cavity walls can be filled with a 'liquid' insulating material. This might be mineral wool, polyurethane or urea-formaldehyde foam (U Foam).

This type of insulation is carried out by specialist firms and involves drilling a series of holes in the external wall surface, removing a 'plug' of brick and inserting a nozzle into the wall. The insulant material is then injected, under pressure, into the cavity. The brick plugs are re-mortared into position with a matching mortar. The insulant value of a filled cavity is increased if the inner leaf consists of cellular building blocks, which have a high insulant value.

If you are building an extension, another method of cavity insulation is to fix mineral-wool slabs between the outer and inner leaf as you build.

Thermal plaster has good insulation properties and will help to raise the 'touch' temperature of the surface.

Floor insulation

Floors may be suspended, boards or sheet flooring laid on joists, or solid concrete laid on a damp-proof membrane—even in older properties stone laid directly on to the soil.

Suspended floors can be an area of high heat loss and a source of unpleasant draughts and dust. While air-bricks must be left free to give underfloor air circulation, floorboards and skirtings must be well fitting.

Replace worn boards and fill small gaps with paper mâché or, with larger gaps, fillets of wood, cut to size and pinned into place. Alternatively you can use a cellulose filler mixed with a little PVA adhesive. Once the filler is dry, smooth it down and stain to match the rest of the wood. Large gaps may necessitate lifting and re-cramping the boards.

A 13mm quilt of insulating material or aluminium foil-backed paper may be laid across the joists to prevent rising draughts, or a second floor skin of hardboard may be screw-fixed to provide a draught-free floor surface. This has the added advantage of being level and a good sub-surface for the final floor covering.

A piece of quadrant—fixed to the floor not the skirting —will exclude draughts between the skirting board and floor. Fix to the floor as there may be thermal movement.

There is not a great deal of heat loss through solid floors as these have a low 'U' value. Added comfort and a 'warm' feel can be given by laying a wood, veneer or block floor, or cork or foam-backed sheet vinyl

Whatever type of floor you have, always use as good an underlay and carpet as you can afford. Not only will the carpet wear better, but it will have greater comfort value.

Doors, windows and fireplaces
Draughts are wasteful and uncomfortable but good ventilation essential. Gaps round doors and windows and chimney flues are sources of heat loss.

While open fires must have adequate air for combustion, you can save needless waste of heat by fitting a chimney throat restrictor. Solid fuel and gas appliances must have a balanced free flow of air.

Draughts under doors can be tackled by fitting a draught excluder. These are of two types—coupled, which fits to the door, and threshold, which fixes to the door frame or floor.

Coupled excluders work on the drop-bar principle. A bar of metal, plastic, wood or felt, fits to the door and as the door moves, adjusts to the floor level. On uneven floors, use a flexible felt excluder. Once the door is closed, the excluder forms a seal.

When fitting some types of coupled excluder, you will

have to remove the door, for the excluder is fitted into a groove made under the door.

Threshold excluders can be used with external or interior doors. On external doors use one incorporating a water bar. These excluders may be of plastic, metal or wood and either fixed with adhesive, screws or panel pins. The edge is usually chamfered to prevent tripping.

Gaps round doors and windows can be insulated in various ways. You can either apply a foam or plastic adhesive-backed strip to the frame, ensuring first that the surface is grease and dust free.

An efficient, easily fixed, draught-excluder system is made by Trent Valley Plastics. The profiled excluders, made by fusing rigid and soft PVC, are designed for a specific location. Four profiles are available for window surrounds and the surrounds and bottom edges of external and internal doors. The rigid PVC gives firm fixing; the soft provides a positive air-tight cushion. Once fitted, the system needs no maintenance.

More expensive, but not needing renewal, is a sprung, metal strip. This may be of bronze or aluminium. It is pinfixed round the frame and then sprung outwards to make a seal when the door or window is shut. Do not forget to fix strip along the door sill.

Gaps between door or window frames and the brickwork can be filled with a plastic mastic pushed into the gaps.

20

DOUBLE GLAZING

It is only recently, along with an awareness of escalating fuel costs and the need to conserve energy, that double-glazing has become popular, as a facet of whole-house comfort. Whether you choose a sealed or one of the many applied systems the initial cost outlay is relatively high. Equally, it is important to remember that double-glazing may not cut your heating bills dramatically, but, combined with other forms of roof, wall, window and floor insulation, will add greatly to the comfort levels in your home.

Glass is a poor thermal insulator. A single sheet of glass, in an exposed wall, has a 'U' value as high as $6.24w/M^2°C$. Inside the home the area around the glass becomes a cold zone. Warm air is drawn across the rooms to the window areas, cooling and contracting, which results in turbulence which we feel as draughts.

A vacuum or sandwich of air trapped between two sheets of glass raises the temperature of the inner pane of glass. Warm air reaching the pane no longer cools quickly and the area around it remains draught-free.

Up to 20 per cent of all the heat loss in a structure is lost through glazed areas; double-glazing makes sense for you can reduce this loss by as much as 80 per cent. Even if the total window area of your home is small, it is still advantageous to double-glaze, particularly if any windows are on exposed outside walls.

It is very important to ensure that your window frames are sound and fit properly before planning double-glazing for there is little point in fitting expensive glazing if heat can escape through badly fitting frames.

Presealed units are factory made, and consist of two sheets of glass vacuum sealed or filled with inert gas.

Before ordering pre-sealed units, measure the window frames very carefully. These units are expensive and an error of even a few millimetres may be a costly one. A 13mm rebate on both wood and metal frames, is normally needed as most pre-sealed units have a 5mm air gap between the inner and outer sheets of glass. It is possible, however, to buy units with a small air gap to fit into smaller frame rebates.

As double-glazed units are at least twice as heavy as a single sheet of glass, it is important to check that the existing window frames are well constructed and sound.

One of the two methods of fixing may be used. Either glaze in the conventional way but using a non-hardening mastic, or fix with beading, which is tacked into place and then painted to match the rest of the frame.

Pre-sealed units can be obtained in a wide range of sizes or made to order for non-standard frames. They are initially expensive but do have distinct advantages over other types of double-glaze systems. When fixed they look just like a single sheet of glass, there are only two sides to clean, condensation and ventilation problems are eliminated and there are no summer storage problems which may apply to other systems. Pre-sealed units can be supplied and fixed or supplied ready for you to fix.

Double-glazed panes should be set in non-hardening mastic putty, to allow for thermal expansion. In metal frames, rust should be removed, as this may cause frames to distort and crack glass. Additionally, panes in metal frames have to be set on small expansion pieces, which any glass supplier can provide.

The other main type of double-glazing uses two sheets of glass as an inner and outer window. These are collectively called coupled sashes. The most commonly used system is an applied sash. This clips or attaches to the existing window frame and provides a second, inner glass window. The inner window can be removed for storage in the summer and for cleaning.

The sliding sash fits in a surround framework which enables two or more double-glazed sections to slide behind each other giving access to an outer opening window.

A sliding sash system usually consists of a side member, sill and headtracks. The fixed position of the headtrack determines the position of the inner window and should be positioned to allow for projecting window furniture, such as catches and window stays. For effective thermal insulation, a 25mm gap is needed between the outer and inner panes of glass.

The hinged applied sash can be fixed open for cleaning or ventilation. These units are available in kit-form ready for you to assemble and are usually a coupled sash. Most coupled sashes are supplied in an aluminium frame while kits and some manufactured units are PVC-framed.

Some makers of manufactured units supply and fix only. It is very important to use the right thickness of glass in a double-glazed unit. For windows of average size, 4mm glass is suitable; large windows need 6mm glass. Manufacturers' units will either be supplied with correct glass for the frame or specify the glass required.

Unit assembly is quite simple if you follow the rules carefully. First, cut the main frame to size and after laying the glass flat, fit the glazing strips round the edges.

The coupled-sash unit involves fixing a removable inner window to the existing window frame. While individual manufacturer's units may vary in small details, most coupled-sash units work on the same principle and can be assembled fairly quickly.

Condensation may be a problem on coupled systems. Moisture tends to collect between the two sheets of glass. To minimise this, use silica-gel crystals, which absorb the moisture, placed along the bottom of the unit. These may need removing and drying out periodically.

Alternatively, you can drill a series of small holes, upwards, in the base of the frame, to provide ventilation. It is still possible for moisture to be drawn through the fibres of painted timber. A strip of adhesive-backed aluminium foil, can be used to seal the reveal between the two panes of glass.

However, whichever form of double-glazing you choose, remember that the price of heat saving must not be at the cost of ventilation. A stale, fume-laden atmosphere or dry air is both uncomfortable and unhealthy for you and may also damage your furniture. Insulation does not mean no air changes, so ensure that you make provision for adequate ventilation.

21

USING THE SUN

Much has been said about using solar energy to cut heating costs and conserve rapidly diminishing energy re-
sources. While some extravagant claims are made for
cost-effectiveness of such things as solar panels, within
the limitations of the technology and the British climate,
solar heat can be used to meet some of the energy needs
in the home—domestic hot water or swimming-pool
heating. Also, the emergence of the still-costly heat pump
can be looked on as making a growing contribution to
energy conservation.

If you decide to invest in these new forms of energy
installation, do buy your products from a reputable firm
which can validate the claims of its products. Some firms
only supply products on a service basis—either to instal
themselves or via an accredited installer.

While vast sums of money are being poured into finding
ways of utilising the power of the wind, waves and sun,
at a purely practical level at the present stage of development, solar energy is the most easily harnessed.

In a domestic context, solar panels—either fitted to
the roof or installed at ground level—can successfully
augment the more traditional fuels supplying hot water.
Such panels do not, at present, provide or collect enough
energy to provide whole-house heating, for to work really
well, strong, direct sunlight is vital—a commodity lacking
during a British winter when heating demand is greatest.

However, as a subsidiary source of water heating, solar
panels are quite successful. They work on the principle
that dark surfaces absorb more heat from the sun than

lighter ones. An area of 4m² will give up to 3kW of useful heat.

In the height of summer, given four hours of sunshine daily, a solar-panel installation can provide all the hot-water requirements in the home. As the hours of sunlight shorten, you will need to supplement with conventional power, though bright winter days will give you an energy bonus.

Taken over the year, in an average UK position, up to 40 per cent of hot-water heating costs can be saved by using solar panels. In milder parts of the UK, greater utilisation may be possible. It has been shown that, dependent on climate, fuel savings on electricity can average from 13 per cent up to 50 per cent.

A solar panel is really a radiator in reverse. The outer surfaces, which are usually painted matt black, are heated by the sun—even on a cloudy day. The heated water or, in some cases, oil, is circulated to a lagged hot-water storage cylinder, using a small circulating pump.

Ideally, a control system should be fitted to control the operation of the pump to work effectively. Individual makers' panels may vary in design, but a typical panel would be about 1m² in size.

Usually, panels consist of a collector plate or heat-exchanger core made from copper, aluminium or steel contained within a robust case. The case should be well insulated to the rear of the panel and will generally be glazed at the front. The case is frequently made from pressed steel, aluminium or GRP (glass fibre).

A minimum of 3m² of panel is needed for even a small household. A useful rule of thumb is to allow 1m² of area for each occupant.

A solar-heating system incorporates a header or make-up cistern of the type used in 'open' central-heating systems, to replenish loss of water from evaporation, although some solar systems are sealed and fitted with an expansion vessel.

Good, commercially produced panels are light and the load is spread effectively to withstand wind and the weight of snow. The inside of a typical panel consists of a mass of small waterways. Panels should be anchored

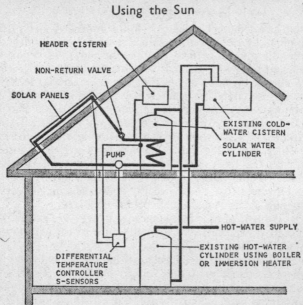

HEADER CISTERN

NON-RETURN VALVE

SOLAR PANELS

EXISTING COLD-WATER CISTERN

SOLAR WATER CYLINDER

PUMP

HOT-WATER SUPPLY

DIFFERENTIAL TEMPERATURE CONTROLLER S-SENSORS

EXISTING HOT-WATER CYLINDER USING BOILER OR IMMERSION HEATER

48. A Solar Layout.

securely with brackets or straps, in accordance with the particular manufacturer's design. A good collector will incorporate fire-retardent materials in its construction.

Siting is important. On a roof, panels should be positioned in a shade-free position or at ground level, facing either south or within ten degrees either side of south, for maximum sun absorption.

The panels should ideally be angled at 50° to the ground, though an angle as low as 30°, and sometimes lower, will give quite efficient results, with, perhaps, a fall-off in efficiency of 8 per cent.

A pre-heat solar-panel installation need not be prohibitively expensive and the installation is well within the ability of a competent handyman—but thorough care in planning, as with other plumbing and heating tasks, is vital.

You can make your solar-heating panels, using black-painted pressed-steel radiators, firmly mounted in timber, aluminium or steel frame, with a backing of aluminium or tin foil and fibreglass, and connected to a separate solar cylinder, which feeds pre-heated water into the conventional cylinder in place of the existing cold feed.

If you use metal or timber glazing bars or frames, it will be easy to glaze each panel, using 4mm glass. Panels can be set into the roof or mounted on the roof. To fit the frames into the roof area, trim back the rafters to size and either mount the panels on the slates or tiles or insert them into the roof. Seal with mastic or waterproof tape or other flashing material where the frame joins the roof area. However, use sound access equipment and observe all possible safety rules when working on a roof.

For pool heating, free-standing panels are normally used and a simple collector without rear insulation or front glazing is generally suitable.

While you can fit electrical tracking equipment for any of these systems, enabling you to angle the panels for maximum sunlight throughout the year, the extra installation and maintenance cost is not really justified in the UK.

Cold-water average temperature in summer is 15°C, and in winter 10°C. Solar panels will, in summer, heat 130–180 litres per day to 37°C–60°C; in winter, the same amount of water will be heated to between 15°C and 20°C.

During cold weather, some types of solar panel are best protected from frost damage by introducing a 20 per cent mixture of anti-freeze liquid (such as glycol) into the circulation water, but these can only be used with an indirect heating system.

A new energy-saving development, still rather costly at present, but likely to become cheaper in time, is the heat pump. In fact, it resembles a refrigerator in reverse—but on a bigger scale. In essence, you could use very large heat pumps, or use more than one, to provide entire energy needs, but the cost would currently outweigh the advantages. Nevertheless, it is possible for a heat pump to meet the needs of the smaller to middle-sized home.

A heat pump can extract heat from water, from the ground or from the air, using an element buried in the soil or in the water of a pool, circulating water containing glycol to the heat exchanger of the heat pump along pipes, often made of plastic and buried in the ground. Alternatively an air-to-air heat pump may be used whereby heat is extracted from the outside air and ducted into the house.

At present, it may take several years to recover the high initial outlay of the system, but it is still worth considering as a long-term investment which will eventually pay for itself, particularly with the constantly rising costs of fuel.

A heat pump essentially works at low temperature, producing heat at around 54°C, delivering an output of 15kW or so, and can be used to provide ducted warm air, serve specially adapted fan convectors with enlarged heat exchangers, or supply skirting convector radiators.

It may be necessary, in view of the fairly low output, to fit a double element to the latter to provide given output requirements.

Heat pumps are relatively maintenance-free and give roughly a three-to-one ratio of heat output for the electricity needed to operate them.

Such a heat pump, taking heat out of the ground, can freeze an area the size of a tennis court and several metres in depth. Similarly, a swimming pool can become a block of ice as heat is extracted from the water. Therefore, in extreme weather conditions it may be necessary to operate the unit in reverse by night to thaw out when the pump has been used extensively by day.

An economy in use can be achieved by operating the unit during the night on off-peak electricity to maintain a low background temperature in the home, easily restored to full temperature by day, using a night set-back thermostat. By day, the pump will operate on standard tariff electricity.

Solar panels heating a swimming pool will boost water temperatures even on the coldest of days, and this heat can be drawn off to provide home or hot-water heating. In fact, it is possible to 'win' heat with water circulated from a pool to a heat pump located some distance away!

An air-to-air pump has a compression loop on one side of the pump and an expansion loop on the other.

When mounted in the roof space, a fan sucks in the outside air to pass across one of the heat exchangers of the pump, which can either extract heat from the outside air or give off heat to it.

The other heat exchanger located indoors, gives off the heat to the internal air which blows across it, allowing warmed air to be deflected through ducts into rooms. It can be filtered, then recirculated for reheating. Heat pumps may also be used in reverse for cooling houses in summer.

Stale air can eventually be expelled by an extractor in the kitchen. A fresh-air supply, at the rate of one-quarter of the total internal volume per hour, is needed on average, to compensate for the air expelled.

Exhausted air can be ducted up to the roof and diverted over the heat exchanger to recover the heat. This also prevents the heat exchanger from icing up during cold weather.

Used domestic hot water can be discharged into a storage tank below ground before going to the drainage system, so that its heat can be recovered by means of a small secondary heat pump and directed to the domestic hot-water cylinder. Spare heat can also be directed to a storage sump, usually below the downstairs floor, to give off heat rather like a storage radiator.

Heat thus recovered is, in fact, multiplied by a factor of at least two and can provide sufficient heat for normal domestic hot-water needs.

However, this requires some structural changes to the home, and at this stage the cost of installation may outweigh advantages.

22

RAINWATER SERVICES

Downpipes and guttering are collectively known as rainwater goods and are an essential part of the fabric of your home.

Materials used range from cast iron, plastic, asbestos, zinc, aluminium and pressed-steel to vitreous enamel. Cast iron is the most common of these in older houses.

Holes in cast-iron guttering can be repaired by removing rust with a wire brush and using a glass-fibre repair kit to manufacturer's instructions.

Gaps between sections of downpipe can be filled using a red-lead putty, then painted over. Gaps between sections of guttering can be similarly repaired. Remove rust with a wire brush, and use a proprietary rust-inhibiting fluid if necessary. A bitumen-based paint will both seal and prevent the recurrence of rust.

Modern, plastic guttering and downpipes are cheap, light, easily handled and require little maintenance, unlike many of the other materials. Available in white, black or grey, this is made in half-round or half-square or box sections. The latter has a 50 per cent greater water-carrying capacity. The cast-iron 'ogee' pipe is a cross between a half round and a square section. Deteriorated metal guttering is, perhaps, best replaced by new PVC guttering.

Plastic rainwater goods consists of a kit of parts, components that fit together to complete a system.

The main terminology of guttering is as follows:

Gutter—A section that collects rainwater.

Downpipe—Fixed pipe to drain away collected water.

Stop-end—Section fitted at the end of a length of guttering.

Running outlet—An intermediate termination with a spigot which connects the gutter to a downpipe.

Hopper-head—A connection into which individual pipes feed, this is connected to a downpipe.

Swan-neck (swanneck)—An angled section which gives an off-set or stand off where the fascia, to which the guttering is fixed, is forward of the wall line.

Shoe—An angled outlet fitted at the bottom of the downpipe used where collected water discharges into a trapped yard gulley.

Angles—Short 'L' shaped sections in 90°, 120°, 135° angles dependent on the make. Used for inside and outside angles.

Holderbat—Downpipe fixing clip and bracket.

It is possible to combine stop-ends with outlets. Long and short stop-ends are available and you can buy, among other specialised connectors and fittings, a PVC to cast-iron connector. These are useful if you wish to replace a worn cast-iron section, within an otherwise sound system, with a length of plastic guttering.

Plastic guttering
Plastic guttering is made in 4 metre lengths and sizes from 100mm for half round and 115mm for square section. In planning a new system, work out where the outlets and downpipes must be fixed in relation to the existing drainage layout.

There are various methods of joining guttering, according to the make. The two most common are by lapping, using neoprene seals, or by solvent-welding the sections. Neoprene seals are secured with clips to form a 'dry joint'. A union, a short section with neoprene seals at each end, is incorporated in some makes of guttering. If the

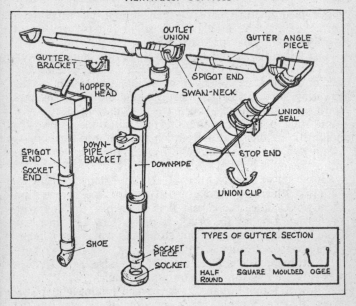

49. A Rainwater System.
   The component parts of a rainwater system and types of guttering.
   You can also have square profile downpipes.

neoprene seals deteriorate, usually worn by grit washed
under them, these can be replaced easily.

Use a fine-tooth hacksaw or handsaw to cut both guttering and downpipes. Cut squarely to avoid the risk of
leaking joints. On square sections, use a try-square to
mark the cutting line. With half-round guttering or downpipe wrap a piece of newspaper round the section. Line
up the corners of the paper and pencil mark the cutting
line. You can also use a section of guttering as a template. Cut carefully, for errors cost money!

It is useful to set out the sections on the ground to
make sure your guttering jig-saw is complete, that you
have all the parts, and that they all fit together.

Next, use a string line to set up the gutter fixing brackets.
Always use safe access equipment and work level with the

gutter position, so that you can line it up accurately. Guttering must be fitted with a slight fall to prevent an overflow in the event of heavy rain.

The fall ratio should be about 1 : 120 or 25mm per 3m run. To establish the fall ratio, fix a nail at one end of the fascia and tie a length of string, the length of the guttering, to it. Stretch the string along the fascia, using a spirit level to ensure you have it lined up accurately. Mark this point. Measure off the fall ratio below this point, fix another nail and attach the string to this. Nylon string, which is not affected by humidity, is best. The string line must be kept taut.

Guttering is usually fixed at no more than 1m centres. Screw-fix the first bracket with non-rusting screws and then work along the fascia board, keeping in line with the string. Do not fix brackets more than 150mm away from a socket. You can put stop-ends which may incorporate the socket outlets, on later.

Most angle pieces used are 90°. These are used either way round to give an inside or outside angle.

Allow a 13mm expansion gap when joining gutter sections. The expansion mark is usually shown on the neoprene seals. Joints are usually snap-fix clipped; these clamp the seal joint and give a leak-free joint.

You may need to use a notching tool on some makes of guttering. This cuts a recess out of the guttering to accept the clip. Notching tools may be bought or hired.

Fix downpipes at 2m maximum centres and join with a socket spigot. Use a plumb line to indicate the true vertical and chalk-mark this on the wall. The chalk will brush off later. This will enable you to mark the fixing points for the brackets.

On a brick-faced wall try to fix into the mortar joints. Drill fixing holes with a masonry drill and plug fix sheradised or galvanised screws. Masonry nails can be used.

Check the alignment between the downpipes and ground level outlets to avoid pipe distortion, using a plumb line or spirit level to ensure that brackets and pipe outlets line up.

Check you have allowed sufficiently for expansion between the joints. As plastic has a high rate of expansion, this must be allowed for or the sections may distend or pull apart.

Where the pipe discharges into a trapped yard gulley, you will need to fit a shoe. Where the connection is below ground, join to the existing service which may be in either pitch-fibre, plastic or salt-glazed pipe.

Soakaway drainage may be to a soakaway or a sump into a highway storm drain or into main soil systems. The latter is not normally permitted and mostly storm water is drained into garden soakaways. This has two advantages: that the main highway storm drainage system is not overloaded during heavy rainfall, and that water from a soakaway seeps down to the water district table—a level from where it can be pumped out and stored.

A soakaway pit for an average-sized home, measures about $1.8m^3$. This may consist of a rectangular pit, lined with selected clean hardcore, with no rubble, or if in soft, friable ground, a brick chamber or pit lined with concrete.

A further type is a pit filled with a random honeycomb of bricks. A soakaway must be capped with a concrete lid at least 150mm below ground level.

The stormwater pipe should enter the soakaway one third of the depth down from the top and extend about one third of the width in and should be laid with a slight downward fall.

INDEX